Movement

Movement

A Memoir of Disability, Cancer, and the Holocaust

WILLIAM ROTH

McFarland & Company, Inc., Publishers
Jefferson, North Carolina, and London

Chapter 16 is from *No Apologies* by Florence Weiner.
Copyright © 1986 by Florence Weiner and reprinted
by permission of St. Martin's Press, LLC.

LIBRARY OF CONGRESS CATALOGUING-IN-PUBLICATION DATA

Roth, William, 1942–
    Movement : a memoir of disability, cancer, and the Holocaust /
William Roth.
        p.   cm.
    Includes index.

    ISBN 978-0-7864-3783-2
    softcover : 50# alkaline paper ∞

    1. Roth, William, 1942– — Health.   2. Tonsils — Cancer —
Patients — United States — Biography.   3. Dystonia — Patients —
United States — Biography.   4. Holocaust survivors — United
States — Biography.   I. Title.
RC280.T7R68   2008
616.99'4320092 — dc22 [B]   2008007306

British Library cataloguing data are available

On the cover (from top left): The author with his sister Evy, dog
Bounce, and father, 1952; the author, at about eight years of age; the
author and his mother, ca. 1968; the author, his son Daniel and his
father, ca. 1982.

Manufactured in the United States of America

*McFarland & Company, Inc., Publishers
    Box 611, Jefferson, North Carolina 28640
        www.mcfarlandpub.com*

To family and friends

Table of Contents

Prologue

I have dystonia, a movement disorder that makes my body behave rather like my cat in that she does precisely what I don't want her to do exactly when I don't want her to do it. For example, when I know my head shouldn't move at the dentist or the barber, it surely will. When I'm excited or stressed, my movements become more pronounced. When I try to explain what dystonia feels like, I usually put it like this: "Make a fist and be sure to keep it closed. Now try to open your hand, and try even harder."

Having a disability is like wearing an invisible plastic shield. I often feel, and am, the square peg in the round hole. Although I'm intelligent and funny, strangers often never get past my jerking head, my slurred speech, my twisting neck and mouth, to discover this. They look at me, think "bizarre," and that is where the relationship ends. Some strangers do cross the border and become acquaintances, friends, lovers. One of my responsibilities is to help them do this. This business of making others comfortable requires a substantial investment of social work on my part and a substantial measure of decency on theirs. And if the invisible plastic shield thus filters out the good from the bad, then I'm grateful to the shield for allowing in mostly the good.

But inevitably, the plastic shield becomes scratched and dirty. For example, at a restaurant, the server often asks my wife, "What does he want?" In this respect, having a disability has profound similarities to being a member of a traditional minority group, to being a woman, to being old or to being a child. I can be variously ignored, overlooked or inaccessible. Such social interactions have been, by far, the most disabling aspect of my life with a disability.

I have built my life and my career on, around, despite of and because of my disability. As I explored the social and political aspects of disability, I became part of the group that established disability rights as a political and social justice movement much like the civil rights, anti-war, women's rights and children's rights movements. Gradually I saw similar threads running through all these movements: power.

1

This insight helps answer the question of why I, who made a major career issue out of rejecting the medical viewpoint of disability, have spent so much time talking about my interaction with doctors. The answer is simple: because I object to medicine as a system of power. In order to save my life from cancer, I was forced to empower myself and become something of a medical expert. I learned to seat myself firmly at the center of the decision-making process and to view medical experts as my wise consultants and advisors. I changed myself from the object to the subject of the medical sentence.

Which brought me to another face-off with power: Wasn't it presumptuous, perhaps even borderline unethical, to write a book about my own life? What about the ethics and movements of memory? How could I disengage the events of my past written in and informed by the present? How could I trust myself to make the movement from the past into the present and back again without creating false lines of logic?

But my cancer changed things dramatically. Cancer made my mind, in the words of Emily Dickinson, "agonizingly clear." Cancer did not make my memory somehow perfect, but it gave me clarity about what I knew and remembered.

And this is what I remember.

CHAPTER 1

Say "Ahhh,"
March 1988

My then nine-year-old son, Daniel, was the first to notice. One day we were sitting together on the couch talking when he said, "Dad, your breath stinks." Daniel was a wise child and, like my father, an astute observer who relied on his senses and intellect. I brushed my teeth and forgot about it. A putrid odor, I learned later, is frequently a first sign not only of cancer of the tonsil but of many oral cancers.

A month later, I consulted my internist about an outbreak of eczema that, like a plague of Egypt, caused me to itch ruthlessly and unrelentingly; it kept me awake at night and left me sleepy during the day. It had taken me eight years to find a wise, caring and professionally brilliant internist in Albany, New York. Roberta Flesh, M.D., was all of these and at the end of our discussion about the eczema, I asked her to look at my throat. I opened my mouth in the ritual performed by generations of patients and said, "Ahh!"

What she saw caused her to exclaim, "Ahh," abruptly.

Roberta immediately got on the phone to an ear, nose, and throat specialist who told her to put me on ampicillin, an

Me, before the diagnosis, circa 1984.

antibiotic, and to call back if my throat did not clear up. Roberta also made an appointment for me with a new dermatologist. The previous one had treated my eczema with increasingly strong doses of topical steroids. Later I would wonder if the steroids had compromised my immune system, or if the eczema was indicative of the cancer. *I will never know.*

Five days later, as the time for my appointment with the new dermatologist drew near, a curious fear penetrated me. There was something wrong beyond any infectious disease. For one thing, my lymph glands weren't swollen. For another, aside from the eczema, I felt fine. Had the possibility of cancer entered my mind? I rather think it had.

As time approached for the appointment, I made an uncharacteristic request of an Iranian visiting professor in the office next to mine for a ride. We walked, and then ran, towards his car, and he drove me to the dermatologist. When I asked the dermatologist to look at my throat, he gave a more panicked gasp than had Roberta and called an oral surgeon.

Two hours later I was in the oral surgeon's office. The putrid smelling tumor was too far down for him to biopsy. He sent me to the ENT man who had prescribed the ampicillin. The ENT man took one look, did a quick snip-snip of two tissue specimens, placed them into a small cup, put a rush on the biopsy and said, "Come back in two days."

Something was wrong. I knew it.

CHAPTER 2

Escape from Vienna, 1938–1945

I was the kind of baby of whom Winston Churchill spoke when he said that all babies look like him. I was conceived in 1941 just before America entered World War II, and was rocking in my mother's womb as her parents were boarding the last passenger ship out of Tokyo before the attack on Pearl Harbor. I was born on June 1, 1942, in St. Raphael's Hospital in New Haven, Connecticut, where my father had interned.

Playmate of unfathomable power and unspeakable evil, even as I wobbled my first steps, much of my extended family was being murdered in the fires of the extermination ovens. These fires, the camps, genocide, and the final solution, as well as the coming fire of the atomic cataclysm, burned into my early consciousness.

My first memory is of me with a wool plaid blanket with thick round fringes on a train heading for Texas. My mother and sister and I were bound for San Antonio to meet my father who was just back from the war. He had been posted to Fort Sam Houston to study tropical medicine in preparation for imminent deployment to the Pacific theater. It was during those three months in 1945 after VE *(Victory in Europe)* Day on May 8 and before the VJ *(Victory over Japan)* Day on August 3 that would come sooner than anybody expected.

There I was, almost three years old, barreling through the night to an unknown destination, the man of the family with plaid kilt material to prove it, a little boy on an American Orient Express bound for the Alamo, Davy Crockett, Sam Houston and Jim Bowie. On the horizon, an atomic mushroom dawn and a burgeoning consciousness of the fires of the extermination ovens.

Because of a polio epidemic, for a time much of San Antonio was off limits to me. Later I remember fishing without a hook off a bridge near the

Alamo — not knowing that to catch a fish required a hook — and being driven up a post and mercilessly attacked by ruthlessly formidable fire ants. I remember dark green watermelons with blocks of ice in equally dark green vats. I remember a storm with hailstones larger than golf balls and its aftermath of shattered neon signs.

I remember sitting at the family dinner table where we spoke German and medicine while downing sauerbraten, wiener schnitzel, goulash and dumplings, Hunter's Stew and Jellied Carp as well as the Texas watermelon and American corn that my father so loved. My parents deployed their forks and knives in European fashion, fork upside down in the left hand, knife in the right hand. Although my father's love of medicine did not extend to surgery, to witness him reduce a chicken into a skeleton was to witness a master surgeon.

Because I spoke German, somewhere between the fire ants and the atomic bomb I was tagged a Nazi in the war games so dear to the hearts of little American boys in those days. I had no idea then of the irony of being a three-year-old Jewish-American Nazi some of whose family were killed in the Nazi death camps. All I knew was that speaking the language of my parents was too painfully different and too dangerous.

Mother and Father, wedding picture, 1938.

The way my mother told it, my father was the most sought after man in his class at medical school in Vienna. The way my father told it, my mother was the most sought after woman in her class. Of course, her upper class father did not initially approve of my father, a poor boy from a working class family.

By the time my father went to medical school, the Great Depression had already spread across Europe. As Jews, it was particularly impossible for my grandfather and my father and his brothers to find employment, a circumstance that nearly destroyed my grandfather. My father's mother died of pneumonia while he was in medical school. On her deathbed, she exacted from him, the youngest of her three sons, a pledge to take care of the rest of the family. My father revered his mother and more than honored his promise. He supported himself and his family through a combination of scholarships, teaching a monster physiology class, and by cutting his own classes in order to tutor other students in subjects he had just mastered. In the evenings before they were married, my mother taught my father medicine from her own notes and he always said she was a better physician than he was.

Perhaps like all mothers, my mother was beautiful. She loved to dance and sing and play Schubert *Lieder* on the piano. She possessed charm, tact, a keen intelligence, and her father's stubbornness that she used to good effect by insisting that my father forsake his teaching career and finish his M.D. An only child, she came from a wealthy and "enlightened" Jewish family whose illusions of assimilation were soon to evaporate in smoke and ashes.

A dilettante student of history might easily mistake the Anschluss as the German military annexation of an unwilling Austria, but Austria had already instituted a fascist and anti–Semitic government under which Nazis routinely persecuted Jews. When the German Nazis marched into Vienna on March 12, 1938, they found a population dressed in Nazi uniform ready to welcome them.

Convinced that to be Jewish in countries under Nazi occupation was dangerous, my parents began looking for a way out. Although a minority perspective in the general culture of the day, their belief in the danger of Nazism to Jews was becoming commonplace amongst Jewish immigrants, with certain organized Jewish groups, and in various sectors of our government. Indeed, what was scandalous was that this issue was not all over the front pages of the *New York Times*, not to mention the tabloids and journals of academics and magazines of intellectuals.

Before the final solution, the obstacle was not in escaping Nazi Europe but in being allowed into the country of destination. Although the Brazilian embassy offered my parents visas if they converted to Catholicism, such conversions having been common during the Spanish Inquisition, my father refused.

To enter the United States required an affidavit promising economic support. One of my father's students was an American studying with Freud in Vienna who would later become a well-known Boston psychoanalyst. She became ill and fell behind in medical school. My father tutored her, and her father, a wealthy and powerful banker, provided affidavits for my parents to come to America, even though it was against his anti–Semitic principles. From my mother's family came another affidavit, this one from her second cousins Aunt Libby, Uncle Jack, and Uncle Abe who had escaped the earlier pogroms of Russia. Concerned about the situation in Europe, these relatives started a correspondence that resulted in the other affidavits that supported my parents' entry to the United States in 1938. According to my father, they arrived in America with only a nickel.

CHAPTER 3

The Cancer All-Stars, March 1988

There *was* indeed something wrong with me and its name was squamous cell carcinoma of the tonsil. The ENT man at the Albany Medical Center recommended a panendoscopy and an excision of the tumor. My first instinct was to call my mother. She had been president of the New Haven Cancer Society and, although her experience was more related to breast cancer and other cancers unique to women, she had far more than a passing acquaintance with cancer. After discussing several possibilities, I said, "Let's call Lew Levy."

Lew had been my neurologist for some thirty years for my dystonia, ever since my psychiatrist, Albert Solnit, referred me to him when I was in college. Although he was now approaching seventy, he didn't look it. He was a wise and master physician, and I had confidence in and even love for him. Lew set up an appointment for me the next day with Clarence Sasaki, a head and neck surgeon at the Yale University School of Medicine. Fully expecting that Sasaki would perform surgery, I packed the clothes appropriate to a hospital admission.

Because of my particular disability, I cannot drive. This has required me to develop at great emotional cost the "disability discipline" of having to continually ask for help and depend on others to get me through all the administrative details related to routine and not so routine transportation. In Berkeley I had hitchhiked but Albany is not Berkeley, and now in my forties, I was apparently becoming too old for many people to stop and offer me a ride. The next day my young, oh so young, graduate assistant, Bruce Bailey, drove me to New Haven. It was a clear, bright day and the lovely road took us away from the thruways on a diagonal shortcut composed of many highways and byways, one of which paralleled a tumbling river. I had traveled through this country many times before and now wondered if I would ever see these roads again. I was not afraid. I was too involved in being sure that every move I made was right. One mistake would be too many.

My mother was waiting for me at Sasaki's office at the Yale University School of Medicine. I was amazed how much the medical part of Yale had grown. In the twenty-five years since I had attended the university, it had become something of a national center, and I was soon to discover that Clarence Sasaki was a world-class Ear, Nose and Throat man.

Sasaki was a short man about ten years older than I whose hands were as agile as a good lover's. Although a man of few words, he occasionally smiled at the same things that made me smile. My mother, on the other hand, developed an immediate dislike for him as she did for people who struck her as cold. Surgeons like to cut, but there was something different about Sasaki that I sensed even then. Not only was he a world class surgeon, he was a proficient medical man as well. I was flabbergasted when he said, "In places where radiation therapy tends to be weak, surgery is the first choice. Here at Yale we have an excellent radiotherapy department. If you want, I will call Dr. Son, and he will see you now."

No operation? My house of intellectual and emotional preparation collapsed, but I was still on my case. Without missing a beat, I said, "Certainly. I would like to see Dr. Son."

I walked with my mother into the bowels of the Hunter Radiation Center of the Yale–New Haven Hospital, underground, close to the tunnels in which I had lost myself as an undergraduate. I was amazed that my surefooted mother knew the way. What was going through her mind? I couldn't afford to think about it. Now in her late seventies and newly retired from medicine, she was out of the cauldron and into the soup and I was the chicken.

Yung Son, the radiation oncologist, was an animated first generation Korean some ten years my senior. Although his hands were more fluent than his English, he spoke more than had the surgeon, Sasaki. Soon I would come to know that each physician has his own technique in making an oral exam. Son first had me open my mouth, holding down my tongue with a metal retainer. He felt around the base of my tongue with his finger. Then he felt my glands.

When he was done, he laid out the options.

"You can either have surgery with a sixty percent chance of success, or you can have radiation. There is a sixty percent chance of cure with radiation, and if it fails, there is a fifty percent chance of making good on the failure by surgery."

My mother asked, "Will radium implants be used?"

Son said, "Yes, but an iridium isotope."

My case was urgent. If nothing was done, the tumor that was touching my tongue would invade it. If I decided for radiation, I would be admitted to the hospital for radioactive implants as soon as possible. As my mother and I left Son's office deep in the cellars of Yale's medical center, our eyes met. True to our history together, although flabbergasted at the turn of events, we did not cry.

We returned to the home of my childhood; the home that held so many memories, some of which involved waiting for death. Yet now as my mother and I began to discuss the options, I put these memories out of my mind. I had to be objective. But here my mother drew the line; she either would not or could not talk about my cancer objectively. With my disability, she had always been my ally for independence. For her, my disability had been less a medical issue than it had been a social issue. However, now, as painful as it might have been to her, she allowed me to talk about my cancer and in this talking I incubated many an egg.

That evening I called Lew Levy at his home to report on the day's events and said, "I'm amazed that a surgeon turned me over to a radiation oncologist."

"If Sasaki did that," Lew answered, "I'm inclined to trust his opinion."

In ten days I would go into the hospital for radioactive implants. I'm not sure how the cancer used its ten days, but I know how I used mine. After I verified that my projected treatment was most probably correct, and that the radiation oncologist, Son, and the surgeon, Sasaki, were first rate, I called Lew Levy and asked to see him. Lew's office was then located between Yale College and the Yale Medical School where he was, as my father had been, a clinical professor. A long time colleague of my mother and father, Lew now did what my father would have done, except I must confess, better. My father did not like to go outside the circle of those physicians he knew well but Lew had no such compunctions. Many times during the following months and years, he would do what he did now; he made calls, talked to colleagues, and read. Lew was as handy with a library as with a telephone. "I will have to make myself smart on that," he'd say and then would proceed to do exactly that.

Now, sitting in those worn leather chairs in his consultation room, we talked. We talked about his daughter who had become a neurologist. Father and daughter now shared the same office, as my father had wished with my sister and as I had once dreamed of doing with my father. We talked about Lew and about his wife, who had been my mother's patient, and we talked about my mother, and about me. My gratitude to Lew is overwhelming. I didn't realize it then, but I was beginning to assemble a team that would do battle against my cancer — an All-Star Team. First base: neurologist Lewis Levy. Second base: surgeon Clarence Sasaki. On third: radiation oncologist Yung Son.

CHAPTER 4

Ashes and Dreams, 1938–1945

My parents set about securing employment. My mother was offered an internship at the New York Infirmary for Women only after assuring them she was quite capable of handling her diaphragm and being forced to sign a promise not to get pregnant. My father finally secured an internship at a hospital in White Plains. There they made him work night and day and sabotaged him by giving him orders in a rapid English they knew he couldn't understand. Later he obtained an internship at St. Raphael's Hospital in New Haven, and he remained grateful to the Sisters of Charity for the rest of his life. This had, as one of its consequences, that my mother did not become the director of the first Planned Parenthood Center in New Haven.

For the next two years my parents led three lives. The first two were the lives of newlyweds and interns working in separate cities and able to see each other only twice or sometimes just once a month. Their third life consisted of the persistent grueling bureaucratic manipulations, political forays, and penny scraping required to rescue as many of their family members as possible from the Nazi concentration camps that later became death camps. Only well into my forties did I become conscious of this other part of their lives. I am not sure how I had thought the surviving members of my family had ever made it to this country, much less why they ended up in New Haven.

Uncle Rudi was the first. My parents managed to rescue Uncle Rudi along with his wife Janke, a blood relative, from a Nazi concentration camp. They had been sort of parents to the three Roth boys in Vienna after my grandmother's death. My mother's parents were next. My mother asked for press credentials for her father from the husband of one of her grateful patients. She got instead a letter stating that any article my grandfather wrote would be considered for publication in the *New York Daily News*. It was enough. The magic letter enabled her parents, Arthur and Franczeska, to traverse

13

My grandmother, mother, and grandfather, ca. 1914.

Poland and Siberia to Japan and board the last passenger ship bound for San Francisco before Pearl Harbor on December 7, 1941.

My father managed to spring his two brothers, Walter and Egon, from the dangers of Germany's Dachau concentration camp, and Vichy, France. Walter, along with his wife Hertha and their son Ernest, arrived in New Haven. Other relatives from my mother's side of the family arrived in New York by diverse and exotic routes, including the wise Nunek who came by way of Africa, the kind and handsome Julek who died later of breast cancer, and the tall Nazek with his short wife, Erna, whose sloppy wet kisses all children avoided. By the time World War II began at the end of 1941, about half of our extended family had made it to America or was en route.

My father wanted to enter the United States Army as a physician. In order to be an army doctor one had to be an officer, and in order to be an officer, one had to be a citizen. One of the consequences of being a great physician is that many patients have reason for great gratitude. One of my father's patients knew a senator who expedited citizenship papers and arranged for my father to volunteer for the United States Army as a physician.

Now a captain in the United States Army, my handsome black-haired father returned into the destroyed heart of the Europe he had barely escaped just a few short years before.

Toward the end of World War II, the United States Army liberated numerous concentration camps suffering under horrific conditions. Among these were Gusen and Mauthausen. The liberating troops included field hospital units established to treat casualties of war. But now the hospital units served a purpose for which they had not been designed: treating concentration camp inmates suffering from massive starvation and infectious disease. Within a week, more than half the inmates still living when the camp was liberated died of malnutrition, typhus and typhoid. One member of such a field team, the 131st Evacuation Hospital, was my father, Oscar Roth, M.D., pacifist by nature, activist by choice, with a father somewhere in Vienna.

My father was aged by his experiences and weakened by a typhus that nearly killed him, and when his duties at Mauthausen were completed, he received permission to go to Vienna to search for his father. I have often imagined him crossing the wastelands of a destroyed Europe, the miles of rubble, the empty eyes. At one point, my father declined the attempt of a German division to surrender to him, and continued down the road. In Vienna he asked Marshal Zhukov, the commander of the Soviet army, to provide him with a vehicle and escort. Eventually, my father found his father's name neatly written, precisely entered, and efficiently catalogued in a Nazi ledger: *Armin Roth ... Thierenstadt concentration camp.*

My father left the army with battlefield promotions, a bronze star, and white hair. When he returned to New Haven and described the camps in a speech to the Yale Faculty Club, few believed him.

With rare exceptions, he never mentioned his years in the war. As children, my sister and I discovered a brown photo album with unspeakable pictures inside. My father took it away from us and would not speak of it. It was not until just before his death thirty-five years later when he completed some videotapes for a Yale oral history project on the Holocaust that the much larger and much darker story emerged. In his videotaped narrative, my father spoke with distance and horror about how the Americans, including the hospital team, beheld with satisfaction the inmates killing the camp dogs with shovels and the subsequent beheading of the camp guards. The Americans did nothing to stop this, and my father, with perhaps more concrete reason to hate the guards, could not tolerate it and walked away.

In the interview, my father showed that same photo album and said he kept the album to prove to himself and to others the existence of the horrors. The first pages are pages of innocence, the trip to England on the *Queen Elizabeth* in wartime garb as a troop ship, my father in the English countryside where the Americans were staging for D-Day, and relatives living in England. Here innocence stops abruptly. Now the photos are of skeleton inmates of the camp; ovens; bulldozers pushing mountains of bodies into mass graves.

Nazi police dogs and Nazi officers, one strung up on a barbed wire fence, his foot and head hacked off.

Other photographs show my father slouched out on the wall of Berchtesgarten, Hitler's Bavarian country retreat. Under each photograph, in my father's elegant European hand, white on black, are written factual captions. The glue on the small black corners that held the photographs has given way and a few photographs are missing. Tucked into the album is a clipping from the New Haven *Register* announcing that Oscar Roth, M.D., was awarded the bronze star for being in the hospital unit that liberated the concentration camp Mauthausen.

In clearing out my father's papers after his death in 1981, my sister came upon five 8½" × 11" single-spaced typewritten pages folded in four, curling at the edges. It was the confession of Franz Zieris, the commandant of Mauthausen, Gusen and other satellite concentration camps. Zieris, on his deathbed at the 131st Evacuation Hospital at Gusen, is described as having been "shot in the back while attempting to escape." Apparently he gave his confession in exchange for a promise that his wife and children would not be harmed. Zieris died of his wounds on Thursday, the 24th of May 1945, in the Gusen Camp Hospital.

A narrative of horror flows over the yellowed pages. Phrases jump from the closely-typed lines: gas rooms, gassings ... seven hundred naked prisoners sprayed with ice-cold water at 12° frost several hours outdoors ... several hundred prisoners murdered by intravenous injections with gasoline, hydrogen (40ccm), etc. Several hundred operations without any reason ... cutting away the brain, stomach, liver or other interiors ... beatings ... starvation ... gas ... one-and-a-half million murdered. A transport of 6,000 women and children without food or blankets in open cattle carriages for ten days on the railway in December 1943, in an icy cold. Twenty-five hundred prisoners from Auschwitz sprayed with cold water in winter and sent naked or in only underwear to Gusen. No food ... secret order ... crematoria staff liquidated every three weeks by shooting in the back ... Mauthausen — 24,000; Gross Ramming — 3,000; Gusen 1 & 2 —12,000; Ebensee —12,000; Eisenerz — 500, Schwechat — 4,000, Linz 1 — 5,000, Linz 2 — 500, Schloss Lindt — 20; Sauerwerke — 2,000; Zerhberg — 500; Loebelpass — 2,000. Transport of 60,000 Jews expected ... only a little fraction arrive; 4–5,000 Jews expected ... 180 arrive; eight mobile crematoria constantly in action ... between 1,500 and 2,000 bodies a day. S.S. doctor, Sturmbenfuehrer and Dr. Kirchner, psychiatrist, killed a great number ... mad ... men of inferiority ... average of 20,000 prisoners during one-and-a-half years. Four million gassed. Warsaw, Kowno, Riga and Libau. About ten million murdered.

In addition to the photo album and the confession among my father's papers, there was a poem entitled "To Be a Musselman" written by Heinz Fass, one of the inmates and a poet of considerable literary accomplishment. The actual poem is handwritten on cheap paper in an elegant Continental script and includes lines like *The noon bell rings, and you stand in line... Retrieve your soup with trembling hand... Sometimes you would like to see the face of your mother.*

Finally, there was a portrait of my father painted by Aldo Carpi, an artist who later became director of Milan's Brera Academy. Carpi had been equipped with paint and canvas by the SS and indeed perhaps survived by painting pictures for them. My father told me only that a concentration camp inmate painted his portrait with a large brush in less than ten minutes. The portrait hung in my room when I was a child and hangs now in my home. Sometimes still I study it, particularly the eyes, which are strange and not the warm, loving eyes of the father I knew.

My family, Jewishness, World War II, the Holocaust — all is mixed in a brew whose vapors mixed with those of Hiroshima and Nagasaki and cast the spell of my childhood. Every month I hear that a family friend who is part of this history has died. Soon the witnesses will all have died. The historical revisionism of Reagan at Bitberg and of a new generation of German historians and American amnesiacs threatens the past and our memories.

I feel these threats as personal.

CHAPTER 5

Can't Help Glowing, March 1988

With ten days to radiation, I invited a nest of relatives to my mother's New Haven home for a kind of before the fact funeral. Some relatives were living in New Haven. My wife, Judith, and son, Daniel, came down from Albany. My sister, Evy, came up from Washington with her husband, Andre, and their eleven-year-old daughter, Simone.

Evy got out of the car with a determined look that said she would deal with anything that came. We gave each other a tight hug there on the front lawn where we had played as children. The silver maple with new buds stood as witness. Even though it was still March, we had no need for coats; our arms were warm around each other.

"I love you," I said.

"I love you," said Evy.

That was the first time that we ever said this to each other.

When I was an older child, I had teased Evy unmercifully. Since I was the "privileged" disabled child, she could not fully retaliate. I exploited this advantage to full and cruel effect. On mature reflection, I understood I had teased her to prevent the too intense pain of unexpressed love. Even though I had loved her all along, it was good to actually say the words "I love you."

Then she said, "Of all people, why did this have to happen to you, Billy?"

Her question astonished me. Through all my years of disability, I had never asked, "Why me?" As logical a question was "Why not me?" It *was* me — a fact. I do not question facts. This is not resignation; it is reality. And although I did not ask the question about my cancer, I suddenly knew the answer. "Because," I said, "of all people in this family, I'm the one who can do it."

These were no idle words. I was the only one in the family who had spent a lifetime getting in shape for such a big match and I was at the top of my game.

Such a simple statement: "I love you." Yet, I had waited much too long to say it to my sister as I had waited much too long to say it to my father. Sometimes it takes death to get us there. Death is exactly what it had taken just six years earlier when my father had called me one night and said in a short and matter of fact way, "I'm going into the hospital, and I'm going to go all the way with it and have bypass surgery." This from the medical cardiologist then opposed to bypass surgery in general.

I well remember the long snowy drive from Albany to New Haven and going to see my father at the hospital. Christmas decorations festooned the cardiac intensive care unit that he had created. A balloon catheter having relieved the exquisite pain of his angina, his face was pink, and he looked relaxed and happy.

He was scheduled for invasive diagnostic catheterization in preparation for bypass surgery. The next day he was catheterized. Dr. Fazzone came out and said, "We can't do bypass surgery. It would be useless. The left ventricle is shot."

His words were a death sentence.

My father was privileged to die more or less at home in the coronary intensive care unit he had founded in St. Raphael's Hospital, tended by younger physicians and nurses whom he had taught. While he was on his deathbed, cardiology residents consulted with him about patients. He had racially integrated the coronary nursing staff, and a black nurse visited him with her pastor. As they sang a hymn and prayed over him, I watched the heart monitor over my father's bed show his heart rate double in response to the hymn. Later, in the dining room, my sister overheard the staff at the next table wondering who was taking care of Dr. Roth. Someone replied, "Who else? Dr. Roth."

One afternoon, I was alone with my father in his hospital room. With its artificial lights and sterile environment, a stranger might have considered my father's room a cold hospital room. But to me it brought warm childhood memories of making rounds with my father. It was just the two of us, holding hands and looking into each other's eyes. His clear green eyes were without their usual glasses.

"I love you, Daddy."

"I love you, Billy."

Damn. It was the first time. I was almost forty years old and it was the first time. At that moment, I vowed I would never again wait to say "I love you."

My father died one week later. He died applying his knowledge and intelligence to his own death. Some two thousand people came to the memorial service. I gave the eulogy, and although I had spoken in front of thousands before, this time I was afraid. I asked my old college friend, Rick, to be on the stage to read my words in case I broke down.

I spoke of my father's passion for medicine and the care and love he had for his patients. I spoke of the suffering and hardship he eased, the lessons he taught, the love that was in him. And finally, I spoke of his history. "When he was so poor that he was unable to afford to attend his classes in medical school, he got classmates, my mother among them, to take notes for him. In the process, he became a masterful teacher.

"When an acquaintance asked him why he and my mother were spending the first day of their honeymoon on a park bench in Vienna studying for an examination in pediatrics, my father jokingly answered that a future father had to learn about children.

"He and my mother left Vienna just ahead of the Holocaust, and then spent several years rescuing family members. When he was told he had to be a citizen to enlist as a doctor in the U.S. Army, he found a way and became part of the troops who liberated Mauthausen concentration camp at the end of the war."

Towards the end of the eulogy, I said, "His life was exemplary. In every difficulty, he sought the life-giving response. The lesson of his life was that it is possible to persevere, to prevail and to triumph."

With each word, my speech, which sometimes halted under stress, became more eloquent, and it was not just I who spoke, but my father. And in this is a tragedy and a mystery: while my father lived, we were rarely as close as we became after his death. Since the hour I spoke his eulogy, we have never been apart.

The family that encircled my father during his crisis now closed ranks around me. Although I have never been a big fan of weekends, the weekend my family descended on New Haven for me was different. I liked people fussing over me.

I needed a large dose of life and Daniel and my niece, Simone, gave it to me. I had always delighted in watching them play, talk and interact in the countless ways that children do. My pleasure was almost poignant as I watched Simone, now eleven, mothering Daniel, seven, and enacting in play a chapter in the life of a mammal. I drank them in.

As I was coming to learn, the meat is sweetest close to the bone, and life is at its best in the face of death.

CHAPTER 6

My Life of Crime, 1945–1950

We dropped the atomic bomb, Japan surrendered, and the good guys won the war. The Roth family returned to New Haven and rented the bottom floor of a duplex on Ellsworth Avenue. My father, knowing more tropical medicine than he ever imagined he would, moved his office to Trumbull Street, then the street of New Haven physicians. My mother continued full-time mothering until my sister and I were both in school. After that she divided her day, half as mother, half as physician who practiced gynecology but not obstetrics, her ingenious way of combining medicine and motherhood.

Since doctors in those days made house calls, my father grabbed the first of the rare post-war cars he could, a Hudson Coupe. When post-war American production was more fully turned from tanks to cars, he traded in the Coupe for a maroon Hudson sedan, a car of character whose front grill bore an uncanny resemblance to my uncle Rudi's mustache. My family continued with Hudsons until we became a two-car family, and my father made it a point to buy Chevrolets and Fords for the rest of his life. In those days before seatbelts, we kids would nestle in the huge space between the rear window and the rear shelf of my mother's green Hudson Hornet.

My parents avoided conspicuous consumption, using their money instead for relatives and charity. Not only did my father never buy a Cadillac, he was modest about most things save his passion for medicine. Indeed, he delighted in defying status expectations by wearing inexpensive shirts and jackets. I remember his happiness at discovering Anderson Little discount suits. Neckties were a different matter since they were the gifts of patients. He wore an inexpensive wristwatch until he received the gift of an expensive one of pink gold from one of his many grateful patients who gave our family many gifts, some of which were kept and others given away.

After the war, I had returned to Yankee Connecticut an ex–Nazi Texan with Viennese parents whose European ways did not fit the post-war image of "the American Way." As I got older, I noted with horror that my father wore shorts as few Americans did then and thought he must be gay, though the words for this in those days were not so pleasant. Unlike other fathers,

My sister Evy, me, our dog Bounce, and Father, 1952.

mine spent his spare time reading medical journals and writing articles for them using his own practice from which to draw his material. For example, in 1948 he published an article advocating the prophylactic use of antibiotics in tooth extraction and to this day, every time I pre-medicate myself for a dental procedure, I think of him.

Although there were males in my life — my father, Cousin Ernie, Uncle Rudi, and my grandfather, Arthur — my early years were peculiarly feminine. I spent my days with my mother and my sister Evy and played with the freckled, redheaded Ruthie and Vivian with the long black hair.

With my curls of long auburn hair, I rapidly became a proficient player of house, jacks, hopscotch and numerous variations of jump rope. Since most of my friends were girls, I thought I too must be gay. One day in Edgewood Park, a little girl fastened her eyes on me and asked my mother, "What is her name?" My shocked mother whisked me off to a barbershop whose Italian barber was forever on the phone. My mother said that he was a bookmaker but seeing no books, I could make no sense of this. I knew only that my mother had betrayed me and that she cared more about what others thought of me than about me. Double-crossed by my own mother, I looked at my image in the mirror and at the long auburn curls at my feet and cried.

When my cousin Ernie moved in with us for a while when his mother was ill with tuberculosis, he caught Joel, our next door neighbor, threatening me. Joel was two years older than I and had kept me in constant fear for my life. But after Ernie put a hammerlock on him, Joel let me be, and handsome Ernie became my hero.

Soon Ernie moved out and I fell in love with Sharon, the daughter of a state policeman, who lived in a corner house surrounded by a prodigious hedge. Hillman's drug store occupied another corner, the First National Supermarket was a block away, and a block in the other direction was Bilfred's Luncheonette.

This was the golden era of my first crimes. Like all siblings, I had it in for mine. One of my mother's dishes from her Polish period was stuffed cabbage. As my mother wrapped up the stuffing, I neatly wrapped up my sister in a Persian carpet and tucked in the ends. I did not want to do her harm, only to send her back. I was to continue in my despicable treatment of her for the rest of our childhood.

In addition to stuffing my sister into a rug, I also lost a quarter, stole fifty cents from Arnold at school, dismantled a saxophone, and began a systematic harassment of my grandfather, Arthur, who told me not to punch his newspaper which made "punch the paper" an instant favorite. Somehow, I got pink Bazooka bubblegum all over my equally pink penis, and it required my mother's utmost skill and thorough medical training to remove the gum.

None of my crimes went unpunished. My father scolded me for losing the quarter, and Mrs. Mooney, the principal, dressed me down for shaking down Arnold. My friend's father yelled at us for dismantling his saxophone. My mother yelled at me for rolling up my sister. My grandfather denounced me as a newspaper criminal. The meticulous cleaning of my penis was painful.

I learned that punishment was certain — with or without an actual crime. I was punished for crimes contemplated, for crimes forgotten, and for crimes yet to be committed. For a six-year-old, I was pretty guilty and so well punished that, with the exception of my conduct towards my sister, I came pretty close to being a perfectly well behaved little boy.

So there I was, a deeply guilty and well-behaved juvenile delinquent who played with girls and dismantled saxophones and who suffered under the rule of a shorts-wearing Viennese father and a crime and punishment Polish mother. Had I been in a Woody Allen movie, there would have been enough material for a youthful career on the couch.

After I finished fourth grade, our family spent the summer at a small vacation resort on Bantam Lake owned by my Aunt Libby and Uncle Meyer who also owned a grocery store in the Bronx. Even today, Bantam Lake brings visions of a childhood paradise lost. On Friday nights, my father would drive up from New Haven to which he would return again late on Sunday evening. During the weeks of the long summer vacation, I had my mother to myself once again.

That summer I learned to swim in Bantam Lake, went boating, released the brake on my father's car so it rolled down a long hill, and played games with boys at the resort. I disliked one of them so much that I borrowed a fiendishly clever trap from a Tarzan book I was reading to dispatch him. I carefully camouflaged a ditch where it crossed a path. I planned to lure him down the path so that he would fall through the covering into the ditch. The lovable Aunt Libby said, "Isn't that cute!" Uncle Meyer disagreed. "What's cute about killing someone?" From then on, I respected him for his discernment.

Many of my parents' friends also came to the resort on Bantam Lake. One of these was Ilse Pappenheim, a psychiatrist who had gone to medical school with my parents in Vienna and who, unlike many American shrinks, had been thoroughly schooled in neurology.

The winter before, my left foot had begun to curl inward. Although not as distinctive as the eye patch of the dashing man from the Hathaway shirt ads, nor in the same category as the walking stick of a dandy, still I regarded my curling foot as a proud distinction and a developmental achievement. That my parents did not share my view upset me. Dr. Pappenheim did not share my opinion either. Nor did she regard my curling foot as psychosomatic, a common misdiagnosis in those days that as a psychiatrist she well recognized.

No, she did not suspect hysteria; she suspected instead a rare malady that went by the name of dystonia.

While I wallowed in my glorious summer, behind the scenes and out of my sight, my parents quietly and thoroughly checked out Dr. Pappenheim's diagnosis. I continued to swim and boat and play with new friends and take many long meandering walks with our wonderful dog, Bounce, whose one flaw was that he loved to chase cars.

One day on one of our walks, first we went east, then northeast, then north toward Emerald Wood where we came upon a small, straight country road. Bounce and I moved on westward. When we came to the end of the road, we proceeded south and then east. We returned to the lodge on Bantam Lake. It was only many years later that I realized that we had traced out the boundaries of a map of the United States. Oh, what glory, what adventure, what pioneering!

At the end of this summer, I took a trip to Boston with my father to see Derek Denny-Brown, M.D., a renowned expert on what today are classified as movement disorders. Boston then hardly had the bustle of New York, but being alone with my father in a strange city was an extraordinary adventure and more than enough for me.

At Denny-Brown's office, I underwent that examination peculiar to neurology. I touched Denny-Brown's finger with my forefinger and then touched my nose. I touched each of my fingers in sequence to my thumb. I closed my eyes, and then I followed his finger with them as it moved. I walked up and down the hall. I performed, or failed to perform, many quaint tasks. The results of these tests coupled with my father's expert clinical history of me resulted in Denny-Brown's definitive diagnosis.

While I sat alone in the waiting room, Denny-Brown confirmed to my father that I did indeed have dystonia, a progressive disease that forces the body into bizarre movements or postures whose intensity varies throughout the course of a day, with stress making it temporarily worse. Dystonia was commonly misdiagnosed as psychiatric, psychosomatic, even classic hysteria. There were few medical treatments, and I would get to sample them all. My dystonia would get progressively more severe. The long-range prognosis held little promise.

What Denny-Brown's words must have done to my father, I can only imagine. From that day forward, my father worked even longer hours than ever and never mentioned "Billy's future" again. But on that day, I had no concern for the future. I ate lunch with the biggest of the big boys and tagged along into the halls of the Harvard Medical School unaware of and unimpressed by its preeminence. For me, my father was a biblical presence straight out of the Old Testament, and I required no further God.

CHAPTER 7

Studying the Opposition, March 1988

On the Monday morning after my weekend funeral party, I headed for the Yale Medical Library to do some research. Unlike the rest of the Yale–New Haven Medical Center, the library had scarcely changed since my undergraduate days. As I read, I began to conceive of myself as an objective case study.

Juicy tidbits floated to the surface of my consciousness like the spots of fat in my mother's chicken soup ... head and neck cancers kill without having to metastasize ... head and neck surgery made abdominal surgery appear recreational ... the end is frequently excruciatingly painful ... et cetera, et cetera, et cetera. Different treatment centers had variations in procedure, and more to the point, different two-year survival rates. I began to narrow my search. I sought to verify thoroughly that I was in one of the best centers. By the time my mother picked me up at the end of the day, I had an armful of photocopied journal articles and a clear understanding of the seriousness of my situation.

I spent the rest of that evening checking out doctors Clarence Sasaki and Yung Son. Bingo, I had indeed struck a jackpot. As I read, I discussed everything with my mother as she moved around her kitchen of gray marble and white tile, a legacy of the previous owner, a tile and marble importer. Although my mother was already in her seventies, her movements were strong and youthful. As we talked, she filled in some gaps and raised some questions. But clearly, she could not share my objectivity. I considered how I might react if Daniel were seriously ill and said, "I wish this had waited until after your death; it's not fair to you."

She paused and answered, "I wish I could take your cancer and make it my own."

The next morning I sat outside of Al Solnit's door with two lumps in my throat, one of them malignant. Since my undergraduate days in therapy with Albert Solnit, I had returned to see him in times of crisis such as when my father died. Former head of the Yale Child Study Center and now professor emeritus with an endowed chair named after him, he was off to Europe later the next day. He suggested that I come in for half an hour at 11:00 A.M.

Solnit is a master psychoanalyst who also knows his medicine. He reminded me of the advancements in cancer treatment and insisted that I err on the side of optimism. He affirmed my choice of Sasaki, saying, "He's made the Yale ENT Department into a world class department."

I was quiet for a moment, then said, "I told Daniel there was a slight chance I might die."

"That was probably a mistake," he said. "Unless Daniel had asked you specifically, it would have been better to just make sure he knew you were very sick and doing everything you could to get better."

"Judith was furious with me. She created a terrible scene."

In the long silence that followed, I took a deep breath and went in for the kill.

"Judith is leaving me; she's drawing away."

When Judith was ten as Daniel would soon be, her father had died of an undiagnosed autoimmune disease. Perhaps my cancer opened her painful childhood scars. I had not been a perfect husband. Perhaps she had fallen out of love with me. *I will never know.* Solnit reminded me that whatever the reasons for Judith's distance, in the event I died, Daniel would need his mother. He advised me to be very careful not to make claims on either that might separate them. This advice was perfect common sense and wisdom too. In the coming months I would go further and do everything to encourage their closeness, including deliberately separating myself from the son I so desperately loved in order to give him and his mother more time together.

Finally, I asked, "Why is the thought of dying before my son grows up so painful?"

Al proposed a few possibilities in psychoanalytical language to the effect that my experience with Daniel was partially one of an extension of myself. When we were done, one of the lumps in my throat was gone. I felt collected, clear, and relaxed. "Why aren't I crying, why am I calm?" I asked.

"Because you trust me and know I'll tell you the truth," he said.

He had gotten it right; I drafted him to my team as shortstop.

The team was taking a full and reassuring shape ... me, my father Oscar Roth, and my son Daniel, baseball player extraordinaire, in the outfield; neurologist and old family friend Lewis Levy, surgeon Clarence Sasaki, radiation oncologist Yung Son, and psychoanalyst Albert Solnit in the infield. Gary

Saxonhouse would play catcher. All were matched up against the cancer. Many of the team did not know each other. Nobody knew they were on the team. The team would expand and change. The cancer was not in our league. On with the game.

My fascination with cancer grew. The oncogenes and tumor suppressor genes were at war deep in my insides. The referee was out to lunch.

Basic science was hot on the trail of cancer. There seemed every reason to believe it a matter of twenty to forty years before a magic bullet was found; doubly unfair that my cancer could not wait thirty years.

I read more clinical studies. As unlucky as it was to have the cancer now, I was lucky to be with physicians of top caliber. High voltage radiation therapy did not exist for medicine until the late 1950s. Surgical technique had improved immeasurably, with Sasaki a contributor.

My fascination reached a horrifying and disgusting peak when I learned how cancers spread from a primary tumor to make new homes in other parts of the body. A cancer cell is shed from a primary tumor and sails along through the lymphatic system. Then it alights on a particularly promising site, replicates and sets down roots. Intrepid pioneers these cancer cells. They create a capsule, a fort like the Alamo of my childhood, to protect themselves from a dangerous body, my body. When they have got together, these break through the capsule looking for new land to call their own. I, who had grown up on cowboys and Indians, indeed had thought, taught, and written on the Western film, could not help but admire these pioneer cancer cells. On the other hand, I had come to realize that European settlement had exacted a brutal penalty on the indigenous Indians and, eventually, on the land, air and water. Pioneering ought to be coupled with respect but cancer cells have no respect. They first violate and kill their hosts and then themselves.

A puzzle. Was cancer an invader from the outside? Or was it, as the 1950s Communist hunter Joe McCarthy imagined, an enemy from within, a fifth column, the ultimate treachery of my own body? The distinction made a difference. If the cancer *was* me, then it was harder to hate. I'd have to fight it for other reasons. The puzzle lingered.

I read on.

If I opened my mouth far enough, tilted my head far enough, had bright enough light, I could see cancer crouching at the back of my throat. If I blew at someone, they could smell it. Practiced fingers like Sasaki's and Son's could feel it. But it caused me no distress. If ever the cancer were to express itself as pain, it would win. To feel it would be to have lost. I would feel only the treatment: radiation, surgery, or chemotherapy. I would have to remember: the pain would come not from the cancer but from the cure.

Although I did not realize it then, I was splitting in two. One Bill was cold, rational, and fascinated; the other was human and sick. Splitting was an important survival skill for me in certain extreme situations. I had made this sort of split before when guns were pointed at me, when I was almost suffocated by tear gas, when I had helped someone in a situation of danger.

And so, when my double went to the library, I tagged along for the ride.

That I had cancer of the tonsil was strange. I was young for it. I do not smoke, and drink only occasionally. My father fought against smoking much earlier than most medical people and forbade smoking in the house. When we did smoke, my sister, cousins and I scurried about in the bushes or in the cellar. Growing up, there was no alcohol to be had in the house except on special holidays, when as appropriate, wines materialized. In later days when I did drink, I drank straight bourbon at the bottom of a tall glass so as not to spill it during a dystonic movement. Perhaps the concentrated doses of bourbon caused the cancer. *I will never know.*

I have not brushed my teeth religiously, nor for that matter have I practiced my faith religiously. I inhabited a dust filled house during its renovation. It is also true that, when editing, I hold a Bic plastic pen in my teeth. Perhaps one of these things caused the cancer. *I will never know.*

More likely, the cancer is idiopathic, which means that nobody knows what caused it — or else it is a legacy of ten years of intermittent smoking. Yet, I stopped smoking some five years before the cancer. That should have been enough. But I suppose smoking is the most likely candidate for prime number one carcinogen. *I will never know.*

By the end of my days in the Yale Medical Library, I knew enough to ask intelligent questions. How was the cancer staged? What was the half-life of the iridium isotope seeds that were to be implanted in the tumor? How powerful was the linear accelerator that would be targeted at my neck? What were my odds? Only later did I come to realize how few people think rationally about odds, risk and probability. This is surprising in a country of baseball fans.

In the evenings after my days in the library, I sat in the kitchen with my mother and talked. She filled in some gaps. In some ways, my knowledge of at least my own cancer was starting to outstrip hers. Perhaps it was because that even though she was incredibly good at the profession of medicine, she refused to act as a physician to members of her family. My father had never had such compunctions. Or, it was possible that as much as my mother was an expert on cancer, my cancer was sufficiently different with sufficiently different problems about which I was becoming something of an expert.

One evening, at the hour of sunset my mother loved so much, she said,

"I don't see how you can stand to study it and find out so much about it," then added, "I suppose that is your way."

She was right; it was my way.

"I can't do otherwise." I said.

CHAPTER 8

The Wonder Years, 1950–1955

I was eight years old and just heading into third grade when we moved to a comfortable between-the-wars neighborhood near the athletic fields of Yale. Seven Alden Avenue was a beautiful beige Georgian stucco with a huge silver maple on the front lawn. Although my mother had selected the house and its location with great care and thought as to her desires and her family's future needs, as my grandfather described it, my mother's new dream house was in Siberia.

On our first day in the new neighborhood, the front door bell chimed. I opened the door and a boy, a big gum-chewing kid, stood there with a baseball glove on his left hand. He looked me up and down and asked, "You know how to play baseball?"

I was too dumb to say anything but, "No."

"You'll learn," said Lewis Grillo and walked off whistling.

As he reached the corner, he put two fingers to his mouth and let out a whistle louder than I thought possible. It was September of 1950. I was in America, land of opportunity and baseball, home of the brave and of boys. Hot dog!

The second day on Alden Avenue I played in my first baseball game. I was not very good and was rapidly placed at right field where boys hit almost no balls. I remained a right fielder throughout childhood and adolescence. I was equally terrible in other sports and longed for the days of playing with girls. Since sports played a significant role in my new neighborhood, I learned early the social subtleties of being an outsider.

At the start of fourth grade, my dystonia began to reveal itself like a connect-the-dot puzzle describing a mythical animal whose disabled outline became evermore my own body. The first dot was my left foot, which from time to time started turning ever so slightly inward. I looked at it, marveled,

and played with my new limp. Was it my imagination or a month later had
the turning inward become more constant and pronounced? It was hard to
tell because throughout the course of the day my foot would curl and uncurl
and curl again. When it was curled, I walked on the side of my foot. When
I was asleep, the curl disappeared.

The next dot came several months later when I lost control of my right
hand, which knocked out my ability to write. My fourth grade teacher, the
lovely Miss Hassinger, kindly pretended to read my scribbling. The head of
Special Education in New Haven advised my mother to do everything possible to keep me out of Special Education classes. This sound advice resulted
in my having a "mainstreamed" education with able-bodied students —
unusual for that time and long before the advent in 1975 of the Federal legislation with that intent, the Education for All Handicapped Children Act.

My outstanding fifth grade teacher firmly recommended that I use a
portable typewriter. This idea too was revolutionary at the time: a machine
in the classroom? How disruptive, yet how functional. I was duly fitted out
with this state of the art technology, and in fifth, sixth and seventh grade I
operated a typewriter with my left hand steadied by curling its thumb around
the edge of the desk.

Dot. Dot. Dot. The dystonia progressed up my right arm, which became

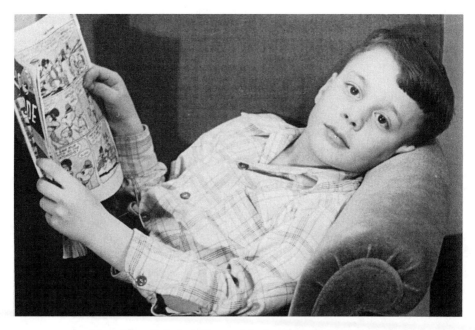

Me, with a slight bend in my right hand, at about 8 years old.

rigidly bent at the elbow and then jumped over to the rest of my left leg making it rigid at the knee. And while I knew the changes in my body were not typical, I accepted them as part of my growing up.

As my mother and father came to terms with Denny-Brown's diagnosis, it seemed the battles to be fought were no longer medical battles. The battles were overwhelmingly social — my education, my playing with peers, in general, my interaction with others. Although they did have occasional disagreements about me, for the most part, my father left the peculiar daily difficulties of bringing up a disabled child to my mother.

My mother became variously my ally and lieutenant. She was determined that I would live as normal a life as possible. While she protected me from a special education system that would have damaged me in the name of benevolence, she also refused to allow me to get away with anything. In short, she created a set of conditions that allowed me to be sane under insanely difficult conditions; a stroke of luck I later discovered was not shared by some other children with serious disabilities.

My mother was one of the few people close enough to my father to disagree with him and prevail. Once after I totaled my 24-inch bicycle in a traffic accident, my father felt it only prudent that I lead a bikeless life. My mother insisted that I get a new bicycle.

Lightning struck. I got my new 26-inch metallic green bike. On weekdays, I rode "Lightning" to school where everyone was on a first name basis with Tom Ryan the policeman and crossing guard who looked so splendid in his neatly pressed blue uniform. After school, I played with the other boys on my block on Alden Avenue. My favorite game was twilight hide-and-seek. As only neighborhood kids can, we knew every inch of the whole block. Since it was possible to hide and never be found in such a vast area, the art was to hide so deviously so as to be found last but not so deviously as to never be found.

My early life was marked off by the progress of my dystonia as much as by birthday parties, school years, and the seasons. Although my stigmatizing lack of skill at sports was mainly due to my dystonia, it also had something to do with motivation. One day I was playing right field during a game of punch ball, a co-ed school yard variant of baseball in which the batter punches a large, air-filled rubber ball. When our team left the field with me limping behind, a small, quick rodent of a boy stuck out his rear end and mimicked my limp. Then right in front of my disbelieving eyes, he stuck out his tongue at me. But what really got me was that he was from my own team!

I was so mad that when I got to bat, I punched the ball out of the park for the longest hit on record for a sixth-grader. On the way to home plate, I

trotted past Sharon O'Brasky's magnificent hairy arms and noted with satisfaction Rat Boy's dumbfounded expression. Everyone was dumbfounded.
Even I was dumbfounded. I returned to my seat knowing that I could hit
home runs. I simply had never been that interested.

In the same way, when I had walked into second grade not being able
to read, my first wonderful teacher, Mrs. Pendar, recognized that while I was
not interested in Dick, Jane, and Spot, I *was* interested in zoology. She gave
me a book about animals and within two weeks I was the best reader in class.

While dystonia progressed, puberty galloped. By the time I was twelve,
I had perused all the books in my mother's gynecology library as well as my
grandfather's large library on subjects sexual. I knew in detail the positions
of intercourse, had studied the pictures in the groundbreaking three-volume
sex encyclopedia of Magnus Hirschfeld and had been brainwashed by van de
Velde into thinking that pleasing the woman was all-important. This made
me a walking — or more accurately — a staggering authority on matters sexual.

Although I was an all-theory-and-no-practice authority, from the
moment I patiently explained to a tearful Susan Chess and her friends why
she had blood in her panties and what a period was, I became the class teacher
in a subject of paramount importance. But when Susan Chess invited me to
her birthday party where "spin the bottle" would be a favorite game, I arranged
for an urgent visit to my pediatrician who, of course, could find nothing
wrong with my ears.

In short, I knew enough about sex to be deeply afraid of it, partly for
its normal adolescent sake, and partly because the changes in my body caused
by the dystonia promised to make sex even more complicated.

Dot by dot, the promise was kept. When my sixth grade teacher
confirmed my fear of girls and sex by assuming that a boy cripple ought not
participate in the class square dance, I learned her lesson well and thereafter
avoided every possible encounter with girls. As girls evolved into ever more
mysterious and frightening sexual figures, I resolved that the next year in seventh grade I would go to Hopkins Grammar School, the all-boys' prep school
up the street.

By the end of sixth grade, I found myself increasingly unable to climb
fences, increasingly dispensable in touch football, even increasingly dispensable in playing right field. I looked — and felt — different. With puberty and
adolescence ahead, my life changed and my social life became far more
difficult. I made few friends, Jeffrey Katz taunted me, and party invitations
ceased. As I became estranged from the world, I became estranged too from
my own body and its tears, laughter, and other emotions. When at the end

of sixth grade I turned thirteen, my father insisted I make my Bar Mitzvah. I learned the proper prayers from Rabbi Klein, a patient of my father's, picked out my first suit — not blue or black — but tan — and had my Bar Mitzvah in front of relatives and my parents' friends with no friends of my own as witness.

My father is a larger than life hero in my mind. This is not hero worship. This is my father's true size. I adored my father and know I can never be like him. When as a child I heard the story of Atlas bearing the world on his shoulders, I pictured my broad-shouldered father shaving in his sleeveless undershirt. Later, I could well believe the story once told me of some Nazis who disrupted an anatomy class and attacked the Jewish students. My physically powerful father dashed down the stairs of the amphitheater, seized a human femur from the anatomy table and knocked out some half dozen Nazis before he was downed.

A master cardiologist and man of principle and loyalty, my father worked from seven o'clock in the morning to nine o'clock at night on weekdays and made hospital rounds on Saturdays and Sundays. Every night he got calls from the hospital and several nights a week he left on emergencies. He suffered frequent severe migraines that were in later years augmented by an exquisite angina.

Wherever we went, my father was treated with respect and deference. Nurses, interns and medical students at Yale viewed him as a master teacher. His patients trusted him and some even called him "Father."

My father was a perfect example of what Bill Cosby calls the genius of fatherhood. Around the house he knew how to do nothing. He was a domestic boob. When forced to change a light bulb he would stand on a rubber pad and wear rubber surgical gloves. When my mother and he took my sister to her first day at college, he cut the wire of her pole lamp to install a switch in the line without unplugging the cord. My sister achieved instant notoriety as the daughter of that boob who had blown the electricity on the whole campus. According to Bill Cosby, all this was part of a clever plan to avoid responsibility at home.

His plan worked.

Mother did the heavy lifting of family and social life. Around the house and in the family, she ran the show. She dealt equally with the great and small world, with the Holocaust and housework, public and private, medicine and matzo ball soup. In her professional life, she was an accomplished physician and pioneer in the faithful combination of pathology and gynecology, saving many women from cancers. A woman of social vision, she created her own form of feminism before American feminism had created itself. A woman and a Jew in an anti-woman and anti–Semitic environment, she was also a feminist and pioneer in contraception, as well as cancer detection and other issues in women's medicine. She was active in reproductive rights, women's sexuality and women's physical and mental health — territories where few had gone before.

In her private life, she gracefully shared her marriage to my father with his marriage to medicine and fully supported him in his consuming career. She also took care of the house and the home and was the family mechanic. Capable of a good spanking or a good scream, she kept dinner warm for her always-late husband and juggled complex extended family relationships. She was a devoted wife, the family anchor and the mother of two — one of them disabled.

My father played a role of godfather to New Haven's displaced community of European Jews. Because he did not like to leave his home except when medicine called, everybody came to our house. There was the painter, Wettreich, who would always knock at the back door; the jeweler, Pereczman, who mended watches as my father mended hearts; the philosopher, Cassirer, another of my father's patients; the Heimers, Lukacs, Gallerts, Schillers. They all had stories. For example, Friederich Schiller was a fine chess player who brought delicious Viennese pastry to New Haven and who later taught at the CIA (Culinary Institute of America). Mr. Schiller had all sorts of trouble in Austria because the Nazis didn't much like his having the name of one of their famous German poets.

My mother — wife, doctor, and consummate Viennese hostess — made welcome this rich stew of visitors and would produce coffee, pastries, and family dinners at the drop of a hat. Outside of this world, I was an easy target for mocking eyes and heavy judgments. But being at home in that swirling world of visitors was like being in jail in Grand Central Station. Singular in that stream of relatives, friends, colleagues, patients and acquaintances that flowed in and out of our house on Alden Avenue was my Uncle Rudi. He came to visit on Mondays and Fridays and, poor as he was, he always brought me a present, usually a Little Golden Book.

Uncle Rudi was the husband of my father's aunt Janke and the first bald-headed man I ever met. Short, roly-poly and ruddy with a mustache and warm brown eyes, Uncle Rudi treated me as if I were special, and he made everyone else feel that way too. Uncle Rudi was the first relative that my parents rescued from a Nazi concentration camp. They were able to get him out and into this country along with his wife, Janke, who died shortly after the war. This occurred some time before 1941 when the major obstacle was not getting Jews out of Nazi Europe but into this country.

In Vienna, Uncle Rudi and his wife had been close to my father and his brothers. He kept the books for a brewery and was a corporal in the German army during World War I. After he came to America, he worked the night shift in a laundry washing butchers' aprons. Gradually he moved up to the job of orderly in my father's hospital. Without exception, the patients loved him. Without exception, children loved him — he was the only person other than my mother whom I would allow to tie my shoes — and without exception, adults loved him.

Before the United States entered World War II and concentration camps became death camps, the Germans placed Uncle Rudi in a concentration camp. Much later when I asked him what had happened there, he described his daily life, being forced to walk naked over broken glass, and being abused by sadistic guards. I asked whether he was angry. He looked puzzled. I rephrased the question. He answered simply in German, "Why be mad?" Much later in my life, my cousin Diane told me that he would wake up at night screaming.

Everyone who knew him — old and young alike — called him Uncle Rudi. He even introduced himself to strangers as the Uncle. On his eightieth birthday my parents sent out word of mouth invitations that there would be a party for him in the New Haven Medical Society meeting room. Hundreds of people showed up.

In my front hallway there is a photograph of Uncle Rudi waltzing with my mother. As a young man, he was an excellent dancer. But in his mid-eighties when I took Daniel to visit him at the Jewish Home for the Aged, Uncle Rudi had cataracts and could barely see, was frail and could not walk himself. Daniel, a highly mobile one-year-old, immediately picked him out and crawled over to Uncle Rudi and began to play at his feet. To see the two together was to see the extraordinary embodiment of two generations together from the perspective of my third generation in between. Thus, although the two played in the space of a small room, they played across the time of generations and history.

Why be mad? Perhaps Uncle Rudi was right. After all, he was the only one I knew who could transform fried Spam and creamed spinach into a love feast.

When my grandfather Arthur, the aristocratic Pole, moved in with us, he and Uncle Rudi, everybody's uncle, spent much time together. They made a bizarre couple.

My mother's father was, in my mother's own words, a character. Handsome, vain, stubborn, and, I think, at least a part-time spy for the Polish government in the years before World War II, he came from a powerful Jewish

Mother and Uncle Rudi, waltzing at his eightieth birthday party, sometime around 1970.

family in Poland and was something of a snob. He had about him a stubbornness I'm told I inherited. We got into many fights, and he gave as well as he got. For many years I blamed myself for our lack of intimacy until I realized it simply was not his way.

After my grandmother died only a few years after my parents rescued them from the Nazis, my grandfather moved at first from New York to New Haven and then, as he reached his seventies, into our house on Alden Avenue, which he persisted in calling "Siberia," an opinion that I would later share.

When I was six, my grandfather taught me how to play chess. While we played, he told me stories of his life, some with more profound lessons than the fables of Aesop that he loved to read to me. Of these stories, none struck me as much as the story he told of the time during World War I when he was a prisoner in a Siberian POW camp. One day he challenged the Russian camp commander to a game of chess. The other POWs bet all their money on my grandfather, who, it turned out, was not only a chess player but a hustler who allowed the camp commander to win a series of games leading up to the big one. Halfway through the big one, the commander called my grandfather a filthy Pole, which sounds especially bad in Russian.

My grandfather, who took his Polish nationality seriously, was sufficiently distressed to inform the Russian commander, "You are now about to get a chess lesson from the filthy Pole." In ten quick moves, grandfather beat the Russian, whereupon the commander rose and said, "Now I will give *you* a lesson." He confiscated the money and threw my grandfather into solitary confinement for half a year.

This story made a deep impression on me and taught me a profound lesson about power. Other lessons about power would soon come in more personal and direct ways.

CHAPTER 9

The Killing Details, March 1988

Even great life and death battles with cancer take place within the complex and multifaceted context of daily life. Prosaic details require time and attention: showers, bills, plumbers, laundry, groceries, meals, school lunches, phone calls, doctors, treatment centers, treatment plans, decisions double- and triple-checked, breathing, weeping, children. Especially children.

One evening, I called Daniel from my mother's home in New Haven. Everything was all right — or was it? Daniel's former classmate had died of cancer, as had the husband of his former principal. I assured him that I had the best doctors, and that we would do everything possible to beat the cancer. My optimism was tempered by knowledge, realism and determination. I think he heard that in my voice.

After I hung up with Daniel, I called my best friend, Richard Sugarman, and brought him up to date. A trained philosopher and professor of religion, Rick is a wise man with the generosity of spirit characteristic of many men of his great size. Rick's instincts and passion make him sure-footed in complex situations that many would find hopelessly ambiguous. As usual, he gave me invaluable counsel about other parts of my life, which however distracting, had to be dealt with. We soon agreed on which people at the university I would tell about my cancer.

Rick did not play on my cancer team; he took care of the front office while my team played against the cancer. Without him, I could not play the game as it had to be played, making myself an objective case and attending to the battle of life and death. Rick had been talking with Judith every day, and, I later discovered, with my sister, Evy. It was he who had the foresight to ask my sister to be in New Haven with my mother. Evy turned out to be an expert patient sitter who made sure that the nurses took care of me and when they didn't, took it on herself.

Richard Sugarman, 2007.

The next morning, Son's office called. We were set for surgery on the following Monday to insert the radioactive implants, or more accurately, the Interstitial Iridium 192 seeds. Since radiation to the mouth is likely to be hard on the teeth, I spent the next day at the dentist to whom Son referred me. First came the deep cleaning, and then the refilling of every tooth that looked in the least suspicious. A mold was made of my teeth from which plastic trays would be constructed so that in the future I would able to give myself fluoride treatments. I bought an Interplak toothbrush from the dentist, the first toothbrush that I was ever able to use effectively with the ragged movements of my disability. Poor oral hygiene is a risk factor in oral cancer. Did that contribute to it? *I will never know.*

Everything was set. Now I could enjoy the luxury of being a sick human being rather than an objective case study. This luxury, living the gift of life, is reckoned by some to be a "gift of cancer." However, I've never been able to embrace this piece of pop psychology. Cancer only nagged me about death. Nag, nag, nag. Life is a bitch. Nag. Life is depressing. Nag. Life is pathetic. Nag. Cancer is stupid. In truth, cancer gave me nothing except millions of new little cancer cells hell-bent on self-destruction and the destruction of my body.

It was a clear Wednesday in spring when I hopped one of those rolling dumps that pass for a bus and headed home to Albany and Daniel. I used the five-and-a-half hour bus ride to admire the world passing by my window. The world was as beautiful as ever, and it was becoming clear that my life had been worthwhile and beautiful. The lines of a poem I had written far back in my early teens echoed through the miles of my reflection:

> Spring is the season of rebirth.
> Why rebirth when death in fall?
> Why birth at all?
> If we are born to die tomorrow,
> Nothing small in time and space,
> Death will all erase.
> Those who remember, also die
> By all the world and them forgot
> We were not.

As a teenager with dystonia and no foreseeable future, death had been as present to me then as it was now. Only in those days, I had accepted death more passively. I did not yet know how love could flourish in a life and the friends and family that could issue from that love. I was grateful to have had the time to discover this. I was also grateful for Daniel and my gratitude was mixed with longing. I longed for Daniel, not only because he incarnated the better parts of myself, but also for the person he had himself become. Daniel was handsome and, already at nine, a natural leader, loved by teachers, boy and girl friends, and classmates.

Daniel exuded life and was a continual reminder of the virtues of life. He approached the world with the same open joy he had exhibited as a toddler in Washington Park one day when he suddenly decided it was time to

Daniel and me, 1992.

try solid food and jumped into the middle of a pizza that Judith and I were about to eat and began jamming gobs of it into his mouth. A few minutes later he walked over to a tree, looked up at it and said his first word to it, "Ba." The tree did not answer. He repeated the same sound. The tree had not spoken to him first, had not stimulated his response. He just seemed to regard the tree as a friend and to this day continues his friendship with the environment. My intellectual Darwinism expanded. As he had once been a critter of the sea, now he was a primate of the trees. What glory!

Daniel's very existence was a marvel to me. Because of my disability, I had never expected to grow into manhood or been socialized to expect I would become a father. I invented my parenthood seriously and went about it with grateful devotion. Many parents wheeled their kids in strollers long after they could walk because it gave them easier control of the kids. I never used the stroller once Daniel could walk, and I discovered all manner of wondrous things by following him around. Not only did Daniel exude life, he was fearless in the face of reality. When he was one, he terrified my father, no easy task, by jumping off a diving board into a swimming pool. When he was five, he climbed one hundred feet up the pine tree in front of Martin Van Buren's birthplace.

In the beginning, I was afraid of these situations. While other parents screamed at their children, "Come down off that wall. You'll break your neck!" I stood underneath in silent horror waiting to catch him lest he should fall. Gradually I lost my fear as I observed the natural care that Daniel put into such situations, and I began to have confidence in him.

While I'm open to the possibility that my loose parenting might have made my son a nut, truthfully, that is not how he turned out. Daniel bore no injuries and few bruises. It was a pleasure to be able to trust as well as love a child and I trusted him. And at those few times when I was close to giving up to my cancer, Daniel gave me reason to fight. He played baseball with graceful strength and flawless coordination and skill. I drafted him to my team and placed him in the outfield with my father and me.

On Thursday evening, as was our custom, Daniel and I went out to dinner. Daniel chose a restaurant four short blocks from our house. As a child, I had loved the rare father-son days that my father and I spent together; more often I even loved making house calls with my father. Assuming that what I loved, Daniel might love, I had started the weekly dinner with him two years before. I loved these dinners with Daniel as much as I had loved my time with my father. Over the years, Daniel and I had discussed subjects from how do you know that the earth is a sphere to football to school to his life to my life.

This was our first dinner alone since my cancer diagnosis. Years of work with the Carnegie Council on Children were with me now, as was my talk with Al Solnit. But most important was my trust in Daniel and in me. In us. We talked for a while, and he did not mention the cancer. Ordinarily I would have left it unmentioned, but this was no ordinary time. I could die on the operating room table or start a downhill slide that might make it difficult or impossible for me to talk. So I started.

FATHER: "You know I have a cancer."

SON: Silence. (He did not want to talk about it. This might be hard.)

FATHER: "Do you know what cancer is?"

SON: "No." (Still no opening.)

FATHER: "Do you want me to tell you?"

SON: "Yes." (At last.)

FATHER: (Knowing what Daniel had studied in science.) "You know how cells divide and multiply?"

SON: "Mitosis."

FATHER: "Right. Now suppose the cells go nuts. Suppose they start multiplying by the millions. Suppose they start crowding out cells that are doing what they are supposed to be doing."

SON: "They shouldn't be allowed to do that."

FATHER: "Exactly. But cancer cells break the rules."

SON: "How do you stop them?"

FATHER: "Do you know why I went to New Haven?"

SON: "Sort of."

FATHER: "Because I found some very good doctors there. We are going to do our very best to stop them."

SON: "Good. Can I have some carrot cake for dessert?"

FATHER: (I don't like carrot cake and know that whipped cream is good only for calves.) "Waiter. Can we have two carrot cakes with whipped cream?" Deep breath. "I love you."

SON: "I love you."

FATHER: "Your mother loves you."

SON: "I know."

We walked home hand-in-hand through the spring twilight of downtown Albany singing altogether too raucously the theme from *The Pink Panther*. As I look back now, we were in a painting by Edward Hopper called *Father, Son and Panther*.

That night, before he went to sleep, Daniel spoke the amazing secret word he had invented when he was three. It was a word that he, Judith and I used exclusively among us. "—," Daniel said, and I said, "—," in return.

Then I went into my oh so lonely study-now-bedroom, closed the door and cried.

CHAPTER 10

A Hole in the Head,
1955–1960

During the years that I attended Hopkins Grammar School, the all-boys' prep school up the street, it was a snotty little place with big pretensions. The headmaster was despicable, and with some exceptions, like Mr. Preston who taught French, Mr. Bekin who taught physics, and Mr. Heath who taught math, the teachers followed the administration's lead. I gather that since those years, the school has changed dramatically for the better, but that is not the school I attended. I'm not alone in this judgment; many found it a perverse trial.

Although I had gone to Hopkins to escape girls, I did not escape my dystonia. As my years at Hopkins progressed, so did my disability. When I attempted to play right wing in soccer in the school's sumptuous athletic program, unlike the other kids who got better as the season progressed, I became more twisted and less mobile. The seasons changed in classic New England fashion and by the time soccer turned into tennis I had to give up on any school athletics.

Toward eighth grade, as my disability progressed and I could no longer type with my hands, I typed with my tongue. Using my tongue to depress the keys of my German-made Olympia created an unexpected problem. The small quantities of saliva that my tongue left on the keys formed a foul-tasting white residue. When I cleaned the key tops with rubbing alcohol, it tasted even worse. I brought this issue to my father who prescribed Spiritus Frumenti — high-grade medical alcohol — on an off label use. This evaporated completely leaving no foul taste behind.

This piece of wisdom, utterly useless now, is typical of the ongoing ingenuity, discipline and investment of time, thought and energy required to craft solutions to the many large and small problems that come with a disability. Solving these problems proved to be fun. My sister had her crossword puzzles;

I had my dystonia puzzles. When Scrabble replaced canasta as my mother's favorite pastime, I got the idea of altering the keyboard on my typewriter so that the most commonly used and hence least valuable Scrabble letters were clustered low and to the right where the fingers of my left hand could reach them with my thumb locked around the desk for stability. The less common letters were banished to the edges of the keyboard. Years later I would hone this talent for solving exotic problems to a fine edge at the Center for Computing and Disability, troubleshooting and problem-solving the routine and not-so-routine problems of individuals with routine and not-so-routine disabilities.

Although I could not compete on the playing fields, in the classroom I had my victories. In geography class I once succinctly described a geographical region by stringing together seventeen adjectives before its name. I became best friends with the number system. By applying my memory and some tricks to the number system, I was able to do the calculations of homework and quizzes in my head. I got so good at this that within a few years I was able to divide long dividends by long divisors — on one occasion even dividing a seven-digit number into a fourteen-digit number in my head. Of course, I used tricks that, I would later learn, were of the trade. For instance, never multiply by twenty-five, rather divide by four and multiply by one hundred, except on occasions when the heuristic was multiply by two, add half again, and multiply by ten. However, it was not simply memory and common tricks. For example, I never did what they call long division; I added from front to back, and later had a glorious time in solid geometry rotating objects and repositioning them in my mind's eye.

In my first year of algebra in eighth grade I encountered Mr. Luther, a most odious teacher who not only misspelled the name of Superman's archenemy, Lex Luthor, but who insisted that we know not only the answer, but also write out the process of arriving at the answer. He did this not to preclude cheating, but because he was an ass. It was an enormous effort for me to write everything down — especially when, as so often happened, I reached the answer by a trick made possible by my intimate knowledge of the number system. He questioned my intelligence and insisted that I type everything out. I grew to hate Mr. Luther, one of only three people whom I have hated in my life.

Where my father's infatuation with American Art Deco diners came from, I cannot say, but his passion went sufficiently deep so that he could not pass one by. Neither could he resist the urge to string his family out along the diner counters on the bright spinning stools. The summer after ninth grade, at my request, we went for a vacation to Lake Canandaigua in the

Finger Lakes of upper New York. As was often the case with my dystonia, I had more than an inkling of how my body would respond before the fact. My lower back had been feeling odd for several weeks. When my father spotted the diner, I knew that if I were to sit on a backless stool it would be all I could do to sit upright. Still, my father wanted me to sit next to him. I approached my counter stool next to my father with dread. As I sat, my back gave way, and I keeled over, and ran from the diner crying. I cried not because of frustration or disappointment or shame at having fallen in front of an audience of strangers. I cried because at that moment, my future became agonizingly clear. I would never stand or sit upright again. I would become a creepy creature of the ground. I would crawl.

My future, or more accurately, the lack of any reference to my future, was always a tender spot with me. Perhaps my parents were being kind by not talking with me about a future they knew did not exist. Perhaps they felt it would have been cruel to tell me I had none. My father often badgered my sister about her future as a physician — a future she did not want. Although later I understood he badgered her about a future I could no longer have, at the time all I could understand was that he showed no interest in my future.

Dot. Dot. Dot. The slight inward turning of my left foot became a pronounced curl — my foot curled and uncurled throughout the course of a day. Dot. My left hand bounced up and down. Dot ... dot.

Ordinarily, someone with a rare impairment such as mine might well have been dragged around from doctor to doctor in search of a nonexistent cure. But I was fortunate to have physicians as parents who, by chance, were not poor; blessed to live in the United States; and lucky for my early diagnosis. With the exception of an orthopedist, the austere Denny-Brown would be the only physician whom I would personally see with regard to my dystonia until late in my teens when I would actually hear the word "dystonia." And while I'm sure my parents discussed possibilities with each other and with their medical colleagues, I was never directly involved.

With my presenting symptoms, I looked like a classic hysteric. As I was to learn much later, people with dystonia were usually misdiagnosed and sometimes treated as hysterics. I have since read horror stories of misdiagnosed dystonic children undergoing treatment after treatment for physical or emotional problems they did not have. Some were treated by futile talk therapy, others with negative reinforcement, a few others by straitjacket. Although I did not end up in a straitjacket, after my back gave way in the diner, I did end up in a plaster body cast when an orthopedist tried to force my back straight by encasing my trunk in a plaster cast.

You must understand: I rarely cried. In an effort to keep my family together, to prevent dissension and argument and the stress that I somehow feared would destroy my family, I did not cry. I accepted every change that dystonia brought to my body as a natural part of growing up. I did not cry. But now, heading home from the orthopedist with my body writhing within its heavy plaster trap, I cried. We were driving past the Edgewood Park of my childhood, and my mother pulled the car over, hugged me with both arms, and cried with me. It would be many years before I let myself cry again. Crying was simply too painful and destructive for everyone.

The orthopedist replaced the cast with a steel brace. My body was strong, and the continual straining of my muscles snapped the brace in two within the day.

By tenth grade I was walking like a chimp, back bent forward, dragging my typewriter behind me from class to class. At school, I found myself a social outcast, never invited to any parties, friendly only with peers sent my way by school — a lab partner here, a fellow member of the literary club there. Between tenth and eleventh grade when my sexual discomfort was at an agonizing peak, I attended a co-ed summer school and zipped from door to door, afraid that I would have an orgasm in front of a girl.

Since most of my schoolmates patronized me, I formed a particular fondness for the more obnoxious ones. I yearned to be accepted as a member of the Boston University Club — a three-man club consisting of Jonathan Finkle, Joel Perlmutter and Walter Bloch. Although I never gained acceptance, Walter was a true genius, and after I stopped applying the categories "true" and "false" to Joel's stories, found in Joel my most interesting colleague. At his house, I witnessed my first seriously dysfunctional family as Joel screamed tirade after tirade at his mother.

Out in the world, cut off from classmates, friends, neighbors and relatives, I was a social outcast. At home, I felt like a displaced person cut off from the relatives and visitors who constantly swirled through the house. I returned the favor by severing myself. Look, I don't care. See? I withdrew and watched and judged. With that withdrawal, I became cold and hard for the rest of my adolescence, estranged from my own body and from my own laughter, tears, and any other emotions. I ignored my body and my feelings and did the same to others, particularly my sister, Evy. I belittled her in conversation, was rude to her friends and teased and manipulated her knowing full well that she could not do the same to disabled me. As I grew older I picked more and more fights. It was sibling rivalry gone amok. Evy never retaliated.

At home I crawled across the wall-to-wall carpeting with which my mother, in 1950s fashion, had covered our house's oak floors. I handled stairs by crawling up and bouncing down them on my butt. I took to sitting in my father's living room chair and staring out the window at a magnificent silver maple. I did my readings for school in the same chair. Though my mother had bought it for my father and it was called "Daddy's chair," it became mine by default.

In those years, music saved my sanity. I assembled a high-fidelity stereo system from components and set about assembling a modest collection of vinyls: Bud Powell, Mingus, Monk, Miles, and, of course, Bird. Bop became a warm friend. I also collected Bach, Beethoven, and Bartok. From my living room throne I listened to wondrous music and checked out the squirrels in the silver maple. Even today, I can still hear the music and see the magnificent view from this chair with complete clarity.

The dots became dashes; my back got worse as the dystonia moved up my body and took over my neck and began tapping out an urgent Morse code with my head. Follow the bouncing head. My father gave me sedating muscle relaxants that soon became inadequate.

As all of this was pretty difficult to live with, to the best of my ability, which was pretty able, I ignored it. So I woke up at seven-thirty in the morning arrived at school at eight-thirty and crawled sleepless to class. In the afternoon after school, I sat in my father's chair and looked out at the silver maple. I ate dinner, did my homework, watched television with the family for an hour, then crawled upstairs to my room and drugged myself in hopes of sleep. Head bouncing, full of drugs that no longer worked, I often did not get to sleep until three or four o'clock in the morning.

Lying there in my darkened bedroom waiting for sleep, I became a fan of early talk radio. As a kid, I had been a daily listener of *The Lone Ranger,* the good guy who always won his struggle against the forces of evil in a half-hour. I was also a comic book fan, in particular Superman, although I had to hide them from my father who only approved of comic book versions of the classics. Both Superman and the Lone Ranger were important to my biography.

Now I learned all about UFOs from Long John Nebel and listened to Jean Shepherd tell his boyhood stories. Long John was good; Shepherd was a master. When Shepherd spoke of his childhood, it became part of a dream of my own childhood. When Shepherd read Robert W. Service or Fu Manchu, I was in another world. I had become one of Shepherd's "night people."

Although a night person, and a fan of bop, one night when my bopping head was in mortal struggle with my more primitive drive to fall asleep, I screamed out for help. My father came into my room, quickly diagnosed the problem, went to his bountiful medicine drawer and returned with some Trilafon, a then newly invented neuroleptic. I was asleep within half an hour.

It seems that in one way or another, I was always preparing to die. The prognosis for dystonia in the '50s was bleak. Although I knew I had an impairment, I did not know the name of it. Although I was a curious boy, I never asked. Although I never asked, somehow I knew. When several years earlier my mother had redone the upstairs bedrooms, I took charge of my own room. The furniture was black oak and the wallpaper and built-in bed and cabinets were ice blue. The drapes and fitted bedspread with its two rectangular bolsters were a frigid rose with black stitching that resembled spider webs. Everything was at right angles. The molding was specially cut at forty-five degree angles and there was not a round surface in the room.

Black oak, cold rose, ice blue; a place fit to die. Looking back, the evidence is clear. I had designed my own tomb. Several poems I wrote for the high school literary magazine show that I believed I would die at age twenty-four. From my later reading in the medical journals, twenty-four did not seem an altogether impossible age for my death. Stuck in time, I was a hermit of a boy with nothing to grow towards except a vision of a head-slamming death as a human pretzel.

The whole thing must have been impossible for my parents. They had wrestled their lives from other impossibilities, all historically more significant than a child who felt he was slowly dying. I once talked about my dystonia with my father. He said straightforwardly, "I couldn't live with it. I ignored it. I worked and made believe that it didn't exist."

Like father like son.

Shortly after I began eleventh grade, Ossie Pelzman, a psychiatrist friend of the family from the student days in Vienna, told my father of a surgeon named Irving S. Cooper who performed brain operations for Parkinson's disease and dystonia. My father, a true medical man who distrusted surgeons, did not share this news with me until four months later, by which time my dystonia had annexed both my left and right sides as well as my back and neck. By now I could no longer even walk like a chimp. I walked like a lizard. My father told me about the operation and asked if I wanted it.

I said, "Yes."

Seeing the word "dystonia" for the first time in Cooper's letter to my father, I dragged out the medical books: *Dystonia — a serious progressive disease with no cure.* By then I suppose I knew it. A week later, my father, mother, and I were at Cooper's office at an elegant address on Sutton Place South in New York, which Cooper reached by boat from his house in Fairfield County.

Cooper was an astonishingly young and handsome man with a suntan and curly blond hair who treated my father without deference or even respect — a new and painful experience for me. Of course, Cooper *was* a genius and a medical pioneer. Most importantly, perhaps, he was a surgeon. As the psychiatrist who had told my father about Cooper put it, "Surgeons are prima donnas and Cooper is the prima donna of the prima donnas."

After performing some of the same neurological tests in his office that he would perform during surgery, Cooper said that if we wanted him to he would operate. The complication rate was under ten percent. He would first operate for the right side. I would require a second operation for the left side. The surgery would take four hours. I would be awake while Cooper drilled a dime-size hole in my skull and then slowly inserted a probe of his own design until its tip reached one corner of my thalamus deep in my brain. Then liquid nitrogen would cool a portion of my thalamus. I would be asked to perform standard neurological rituals with the hand on the opposite side of where the probe was inserted because the brain paths cross. Finally, when Cooper was satisfied, the liquid nitrogen would be turned up to destroy a small volume of my brain with the object of interrupting the electrical impulses that ran through that part of the brain.

My father asked, "Is Bill a good candidate for surgery?"

Cooper said, "A fair candidate." My hackles rose; his response felt like an insult.

We knew there was no alternative. Decision forced. Two weeks later I found myself in a bizarre hospital in the Bronx called Saint Barnabas Hospital for Incurables. I had never seen so many old people in wheelchairs.

I was lucky and that the procedure existed at all was even more luck. Cooper had developed this surgery for his Parkinson's patients in the days before the drug L-Dopa was developed. He had tried the surgery with the orphan disease of dystonia and it had worked.

One surgical approach to Parkinson's was to burrow deep in the brain with a knife. Sometimes it worked, more often not. The procedure had a fifty percent plus mortality rate that affected its popularity. One day Cooper tried this procedure with a patient where there was nothing to lose. On the way in he severed an artery. Cooper stopped the operation and sewed everything back. Lightning struck. The man got better. Cooper preformed countless experiments on the brains of dogs and developed a procedure where a catheter was inserted into a precise part of the brain responsible for movement.

Luck, luck, and more luck. Cooper had just started doing the Parkinson's procedure on other conditions including dystonia. I was among his first dystonia cases.

I do not remember the operations too well. Though I was awake and sedated, the surgery was not fun. Of course, I had Novocain in the scalp and the brain feels no pain. However, it was not pleasant to have a ventriculogram —

a precursor to the modern imaging techniques like CT scans and MRIs — in which a hole was poked in my spine and air shot up the spine to visualize my brain. Nor was it agreeable to have screws turned down through my skull. Nor was it nice to discover that with my head immobilized, my body thrashed around. Nor were the vibrations of the drill going through my skull pleasant. But I complain. There was no alternative.

Then — a miracle. After the operation, aside from a slight stiffness in my right foot, my right side was entirely normal. For the first time in five years I could write and wrote myself get well cards. My handwriting was exactly as it had been when last I had written as a fourth grader.

In those days people stayed in the hospital for weeks after operations. My average stay was three to four weeks. Over the next weeks in the hospital, I wasted time in physical therapy, occupational therapy, and time with social workers and psychologists. The decisive intervention was already an accomplished fact. While in the hospital I met some other kids of about my age with dystonia, the first I had ever met. Because dystonia is a highly variable disease, I had no immediate feeling of kinship. However, I became close to a kid maybe three years younger than I who was there for the same operation. From him, I concluded that kids had an awful lot of guts. I do not know what became of those other kids. My most immediate impression was that I was the sanest of the children there and that my parents had done an awful lot right.

Finally I went home. I don't remember what happened in the next weeks. All that I remember is that first slowly and then more rapidly the symptoms on my right side returned, until finally, with the exception of my stiff foot, everything was back the way it had been before in a matter of weeks not years.

My biography of impairment was now distilled into a five-week instant replay. My chances of a reprieve were folded. I was not cured nor was the progress of the dystonia arrested. It was more than I could take. Five weeks later I saw Cooper again. I explained to him what had happened and fell into buckets of tears. Cooper seemed angry with me. He had failed in his surgery. "I can't take any more of this," he said. "I will see you in the operating room."

My second operation was not as dramatically successful, but its results were permanent. As it turned out, I would undergo four surgeries. Operation three was also not completely successful, but the results seemed permanent. Considerably better. I now could walk, feed and dress myself. I could scamper. I could even kind of skip. Though I was never able to write and never returned to typing, my hands were usable. Importantly, with the progress of my dystonia arrested, I could reinvest trust in my body. Living a long life now became a distinct possibility.

I could now dream of that thing called a future.

Given my father's distaste for surgery, it is clear my parents were truly desperate in choosing Cooper's controversial procedure. I myself did not then understand how controversial it was. In some arenas, Cooper was even considered a quack, especially as others could not repeat his results. Until several years ago, Cooper's procedure usually went unmentioned or was derided in the neurology books. When a team of British doctors repeated Cooper's procedure, this time with modern technology, three out of seven patients died; the other four showed no improvement. The end of the controversy then appeared to be that his procedure did not work, which made me feel rather like a ghost.

Cooper remained a controversial figure. He made further medical advances and later cooperated in the development of L–Dopa, a drug for Parkinson's disease that made his surgical procedure far less necessary. He also wrote books on his surgery for lay people as well as novels before retiring to Florida at an early age where he later died of cancer. Without him I might have become a pretzel to die of pneumonia or some other complication of dystonia. In retrospect, he was one of a kind.

When I graduated from high school in June of 1960, I walked up to the podium to receive my diploma and returned to my seat. A stranger at the ceremony would have been puzzled at the applause this occasioned. The applause was bittersweet; in all that time, no one at school had ever mentioned my surgeries. Although I was held up as an inspiration, I had few friends. I was sick of being a superhuman inspiration.

If my adolescent years seem bleak, mostly they were. They were bleak not because of my disability but because of its progress and because of my certainty of death and because of my loneliness. Yet all was not bleak. Although I never thought of myself as a good student, I was. My school, ridiculous as it was, was a place where I could excel academically and discover amazing things. My mind, homebound though it was, made many trips. I was a keen observer and from my father's living room chair I observed survivors of the Nazi death camps float in and out of the house. My sanity was further preserved when I learned how to masturbate from a neighbor who, not as a result, later died of gangrene.

CHAPTER 11

Three Days to Burn, March 1988

During the three days I had left in Albany before returning to New Haven for the radioactive implant surgery, Judith and I discussed everything from how she should handle finances in the event of my death, to collecting on my life insurance, to managing my estate. These conversations had about them an unsettling formal intimacy — she had spoken no clear words of parting, yet the chasm between us was already great, and our words echoed off its walls.

Then there was the question of Daniel visiting me. Should they come to New Haven? Should they come to the hospital? I thought not. I would be "hot." My radioactive implants would be dangerous to others and more so to growing children. My hospital bed would be in isolation in a private room at the end of the hall, which became free in the gynecology ward. Visitors would be allowed in only for five-minute intervals. Even then they would stand behind a lead screen. Daniel was starting to ask questions about nuclear war, and I thought that radiation would be too confusing a subject for him. Finally, I did not want to be distracted from preparing for the coming battle.

Back in New Haven, on Saturday evening after sundown, I walked a few blocks from my mother's house to see Joe Lieberman, a Yale suite mate, who that afternoon had accepted the Democratic nomination as candidate for United States Senator. Joe, along with Rick Sugarman, had been with me at my father's funeral. As is Orthodox Judaic custom, they had shoveled the earth over my father's plain pine coffin.

Joe introduced me to fifteen newly drafted campaign workers, a lean group to go after Weicker's safe seat. Someone played Joe's videotaped acceptance speech and television crews came to interview him. I had never seen Joe in this context before and was impressed with how he handled himself.

After the television crews left, the evening turned into a victory party.

In the midst of the celebration, Joe appeared with a friend, saying, "I think you two might have something to talk about," and left us to talk. His friend, Peter, turned out to be a psychoanalyst who had recently undergone surgery for a cancer in his neck. We talked most of the evening and our conversation traveled from Joe's house to my mother's kitchen where we talked frankly about cancer and our children. Toward the end of our talk, I asked Peter bluntly, "There is a possibility of dying with your cancer; how do you deal with it?"

"Denial," Peter said, "I usually pretend death is unreal." And with that, he left.

That night, as I reflected on the day and my life, I was dazzled by Joe's kindness in the midst of his own victory celebration. I realized that even were I to die on the operating room table, my life had been happy, of purpose and full. Still, even if the glass was full, it was too damn short. And I had a duty to be Daniel's father. The cancer was not only threatening me, it was threatening my fatherhood.

Whether it's because my dystonia prevents me from writing, or because I am uncivilized and lazy, it's difficult for me to keep up with old friends. Whatever the reason, that night, I called my friend Gary Saxonhouse, with whom I had not spoken for too long a time. With deep concern Gary led me through the events of the past week. Why had I opted for radiation instead of surgery? How did I know that Sasaki was so good? What was my relationship to Lew? He asked these questions in a voice so loving that I did not feel my decisions challenged. Rather, he led me to rethink them as part of a logical pattern. Like me, Gary loved me; like me, he was able to treat me as an objective case — a lovable objective case.

Gary is a brilliant economist and master of decision-making. As an econometrician, he is also a skilled analyst of statistical information. My studies had included enough statistics and econometrics to make me comfortable

Gary Saxonhouse, 1986.

with probability. Together we reviewed the various studies and concluded that I had about a seventy percent chance of a two-year survival. That would get Daniel to twelve. When we added to that my proven track record as a fighter and the uncommon skill of the Yale head-neck cancer people, I agreed with his estimate of eighty-five percent.

Gary has that rare mind capable of warm love and cool rationality, finely honed in evaluative nuances. I recruited him to my team.

Under a cloudless blue sky on the Sunday morning before the implant surgery, Daniel and I ambled down the streets of my childhood and wandered over to the polo stable at Yale where I had been many times as a child. As we walked around the stables, I talked about the different kinds of horses. "Polo ponies are small," I said. Daniel wasn't interested. I started conversations and left him openings. Daniel lay low. We headed back towards my mother's house. About five minutes from the house, I repeated, "I'll have the operation on Tuesday, and I probably won't be able to talk for a while. But I'll call you each day and look forward to hearing from you."

Daniel lay low.

If Peter was entitled to denial, surely Daniel was too.

That afternoon when the car carrying Judith and Daniel pulled away from the curb, I stood on the sidewalk and wept when they left. Then I went upstairs, packed a small bag for the hospital and slept.

On Monday, in accordance with Doctor Son's directive, I went to the barbershop to have my beard shaved off. I had first grown a beard at Berkeley and kept it not because of professorial eccentricity, but because attempting to shave with the ragged neural outbursts of dystonia is laborious, not to mention dangerous. Now facing me in the mirror was a Samson hairless who smiled at me.

On Tuesday, I checked into my tiny hospital room at the Yale–New Haven Hospital. My mother hung up my clothes and stowed my gear. My cousin Ernie brought in a pastrami special from Chuck's, our childhood deli. The anesthesiology resident came in, and I recited my medical history for the thousandth time. I went to sleep well drugged, not because of my cancer, but because of the eczema that had made my existence almost intolerable for the past six months — and which, over the next five days, would totally disappear.

Future cancer treatment became present fact.

CHAPTER 12

Yale, 1960–1961

"How beauteous mankind is!
O brave new world that has such people in't!"
—William Shakespeare, *The Tempest*

Applying to Yale was automatic; I didn't apply anywhere else. Yale was the local school, and I always assumed that I would get in. Almost one-third of my class at Hopkins Grammar School got in. After all, its motto was "for the bringing up of hopeful youth."

One afternoon I heard my father's voice seeping through the thin sheetrock walls of our summer cottage on the lake. My ears perked up — the call had something to do with me. I listened intently. My father was talking to the head of the Yale health clinic. Out of kindness Yale had decided that, though I had been admitted, I would be better off not going. Clearly, being a Yale man would be too demanding for a boy with a disability, although I was fully capable otherwise.

Suddenly I released the breath I had been holding. I was appalled that some other person would make that kind of decision for me. My father knew the head of the clinic professionally, and as he spoke, his next words penetrated clearly through the thin walls. "I have seen courage," he said. "I have seen courageous soldiers fight against the Germans. I have never seen anyone as courageous as Bill."

These words still haunt and confound me today.

I could not get over my father calling me courageous. Was he talking about my literally dragging myself to school every day without complaint? Or by courage did he refer to my life lived in the face of death? Only this last possibility is coherent to me. But even so, my courage was at most personal. I could not compare it to courage on a world historical scale, which my father had surely witnessed and was indeed himself an example of. Looking back at it, I still do not think I was courageous then — although I would use that term to describe myself later in my battle with cancer. Yet my father was neither a liar nor a fool.

My father did not ask for a favor. He built his argument around courage — my courage. As I walked into the living room, my father was speaking calmly as physicians do in times of medical emergency. When he hung up, he turned toward me with anger in his eyes. "The good doctor said that he would assure the officials at Yale that there is no medical reason for keeping you out. We should relax until he gets back to us."

The doctor got back to my father, and I was let into Yale.

That August, at my request, my family traveled to Europe. At some level each of us realized that between Cooper and wild good luck, I had been snatched from the hobnailed boot of death. When we landed in Paris, I immediately fell in love with the city. Perhaps because it was the first time I was able to walk through a crowd of people without bumping into any, or because of the smells, or because of the turns and rhythms of the streets. Whatever the reason, I came to equate walking with Paris and city life and resolved to return.

Also at my request, my father bought a state of the art Citroen DS-19, a car that went up and down on advanced air bag suspension. We picked it up in a suburb of Paris. My father got one of his frequent migraines and wrapped a makeshift tourniquet around his head. The French gathered to comment on this curious sight of a man wearing his wife's pink plastic sun glasses, with a diaper-like affair wrapped tightly around his head in a brand new Citroen that was moving up and down in place with the menace of a Cheshire cat. Because my father always lost his sense of direction when he had a migraine, he paid a factory worker to drive us to the highway.

With the Citroen going up and down, we made our grand tour from Paris through Switzerland, Italy, Yugoslavia, and Austria. As we headed north from Yugoslavia and through the Austrian Alps, my parents told stories of skiing the Alps in the days before mechanical lifts when people climbed up the mountain they skied down.

In Austria we went to Vienna, simultaneously my parents' home, evictor, and almost murderer. At a medical meeting in Vienna my parents met many pre-war friends, each one made more insane than the other by this angry mother of their childhood. I leave you as evidence the picture of my thoroughly disoriented father desperately driving the wrong way down a one-way street. When stopped by a policeman, he took out his U.S. passport and said in his piggiest pig–German, "I don't speak German."

Back home in New Haven with our new Citroen, we found that it was so advanced, we could find no one to repair it and had to sell it.

Shortly thereafter, on a bright morning at the end of the summer and just before the start of the crisp New England autumn, I arrived with my parents at the old campus, the original site of Yale College. Throngs of boys were saying their good-byes to hordes of parents from all over the country in melodious Southern accents and the nasal accents of New York, never mind the inflections of the mid-west. Within a month the accents would disappear and regional dress would be replaced by Yale understatement: loafers, khakis, and buttoned-down shirts with rep-striped ties, and either a blue blazer or a tweed jacket.

Yale was an intellectually exciting university. During the years that I attended from 1960 to 1964, I have no doubt that Yale offered the best undergraduate education in the world. In measure this was because of a superb liberal arts faculty. In greater measure it was because Mother Yale deployed her faculty in the service of her undergraduates. At Yale the undergraduates were king; the faculty, members of the court; the graduate students and the staff, ill-understood functionaries. Yale was called *Mother Yale* by her children for excellent reason.

At Yale we not only were encouraged to dream of greatness, greatness was a given. Filled with self-confidence, we could learn with bravado if we so chose, that artificially small fraction of us who were Jewish would have used the word "chutzpah." At the time, I did not realize that learning was only one of the options of kings; another option, of course, was to rule. The menu of marvelous courses dazzled me. I had taken advanced English, physics, and calculus in secondary school. But these familiar subjects were nonetheless excitingly different from their cold prep school counterparts. Other subjects were completely new and tantalizing revelations of future intellectual promise. For the first time in my life, I was part of the greater world. It was glorious, and I felt glorious. What luxury and privilege! What an elegant place to grow up.

For me, a disabled teenager so dependent on his parents, the adolescent task of finding my individuality had been impossible. However, starting with Yale, I purposefully began establishing my independence and relationships outside of my family. With great eagerness, I looked forward to living in the dormitories with roommates and to making my first friends. Therefore it was with great horror that I found myself assigned to solitary confinement in a single room in Connecticut Hall, the oldest building at Yale. Yale had ordained me a hermit.

In a move that required overt nerve, I visited Dean Thompson who was in charge of freshmen. My heartbeats noted my anxiety as I told him of my wish to have roommates and why. "You've just made my life easier," Dean

Thompson answered. "Do you know how many people around here want single rooms? I'll put you in a room of four and put someone who wants a single into your room."

"Thank you," I said.

Everybody won. Dean Thompson and I became friends. I got to live with other people. Another freshman got a single.

This episode proved instructive. Dean Thompson had discriminated against me not out of malice, but from a lack of correct information. Now I understood that most of the social work of supplying correct information would be left to me. As I grew and matured, I accepted this burden as part of my role in social interactions. The second lesson was this: people in positions of power who made decisions — even for my benefit — could do me in. They could assume that I was not up to going to Yale. They could assume I was not up to having roommates, et cetera. Thus, I worked on developing my good-natured toughness.

In succeeding years, the benefits of having roommates during my freshman year steadily accrued.

Early in freshman year I became involved with a group of upperclassmen known as Challenge. Brilliant and enthusiastic, they took on the mission of carrying Yale from the '50s into the '60s. Through my work with Challenge, I lived even more of my life in the large world. I took trips to Boston and New York, and recruited speakers for symposia that Challenge gave. The most decisive contribution of Challenge to my education was a four-hour meeting of six of us with George Kennan, a famed wise man of American foreign policy.

I pursued mathematics as a field of study. The mathematics professors at Yale were uncouth or, at least, definitely not Yale. The math graduate students were surly and some even sported duck's-ass haircuts. I became particularly friendly with my teacher, Frank Hahn, who later died an early death of cancer. Halfway through the year I asked him what caliber of mathematician I would make. He answered, "Just about average." Since, of course, I could not possibly be average, I started surveying fields where excellence was a possibility — politics, economics, medical research, and the like.

Freshman year was juicy. Each day brought its own excitement. Each event was soaked with newness. My friends at Yale invited me to their homes. I marveled at the different ways that others lived. One friend's parents were divorced; another had a butler; yet another friend's family spent the day playing together at a go-cart track.

In the second semester I took a philosophy course entitled "A Critical Study of Marxist Theory." Of course, any study of Marxism at Yale launched in 1960 and coming out of the 1950s had to be critical. The 1844 manuscripts were delivered to us on ditto sheets. This taboo topic was exciting; it was another way of looking at the world from the liberalism that I had taken as a given.

During this time, I was astonished at the profusion of flowers that life at Yale offered me — although the roses were not without fertilizer. At meals in freshman commons tie and jacket were mandatory. My dystonia made it exceedingly difficult for me to tie a necktie and impossible to fasten my top button. I had worn neckties throughout my six deadly years at Hopkins during which my mother had done all the tying and buttoning. As I was growing up, I did not realize that because of my dystonia my neck was inordinately large — seventeen-and-a-half. So it was that I was strangled for six years. I attributed this strangulation as a natural property of the tie and jacket that I had come to detest.

Now I took to wearing a scarf instead of a necktie. Halfway through freshman year I received a note from undergraduate dean Whiteman, my first official bureaucratic memo, stating the dress code. Then, as a postscript, it said, "Remember, disorder is contagious." Strangely pleased with the reprimand, I stuck to my scarves and thus began my career in institutional reform and social protest.

All things considered, my freshman year was far better than the dreams I never dreamed.

CHAPTER 13

Cancer, Present Tense, March 31, 1988

On the morning of the surgery, Lew woke me up and stayed with me until the gurney came to take me to the operating room. Then did I wheel through endless corridors, around many corners, and descend countless floors by elevator, until finally I was in a room with twenty other patients on gurneys. After fifteen minutes, an orderly read my name off a chart and asked me if the name was mine. Then, still without fear though flat on my back, I was wheeled into the operating room. Everyone wore masks, which always makes me think of outlaws in Westerns. The last thing I remember is a small prick on my hand.

I was in the best of hands. Yung Son is Yale's expert at implants, as well as a member of Yale's head and neck cancer group. While I was unconscious Son inserted nylon tubes through my cheek and my tonsil and to the greedy little bastard inside. CAT scans, x-rays and dosimetric calculations were made and dummy seeds were implanted. When I regained consciousness, they replaced the dummy seeds with the radioactive seeds fashioned from Iridium 192. Now I was hot. Nurses and guests were allowed to be with me only five minutes at a time. For the first time it dawned on me that the rest of my body would be exposed to the implants twenty-four hours a day.

The first day I largely slept through the visits of doctors, nurses, family, friends, and the visit of Warren Ilchman, the executive vice president for academic affairs at the university where I teach. Warren is an old friend, a former teacher at Berkeley, and a busy man. The note that he left with greetings from everyone in the university's administration assured me that for the time being I could worry about myself and not about work. His kind note made me cry. I was learning that unexpected kindness was moving. I was also learning to let myself cry when moved. And a good thing too, because the next morning when Lew woke me, I needed to cry — and I did. However precisely, a foreign body had been rammed into the left side of my face. Nylon string came out from my mouth and was tied to nylon string connected to the nylon tubes in my jaw.

I asked for my dosage of Demerol every four hours not because I was in physical pain, but because I felt terrible. I knew when the Demerol hit because the little black and white television screen would sink down eight inches. Because I was so high, I have scant recollection of what happened.

After five days it was time to remove the foreign tubes. Son was there, with his chief nurse, Barbara Cutler, who had known my father, as well as the radiation physicist with lead container and Geiger counter, and the floor nurse. Son took a pliers-like affair, easily withdrew a tube whose strings he had previously cut, and placed it into the lead container. The second tube did not want to come out at first. This led to a discourse by the radiation physicist on the design of tube extractors. The other tubes came out easily. Snip-pull-drop. These men were not afraid of radiation. They seemed to revel in it. The last tube came out oh so easily and hemorrhaged at its entry point in the back of my throat.

I coughed up a liquid which I saw to my amazement was my own blood. My throat filled with blood again. Son got up on the bed for a better angle to stop the bleeding. My next cough sprayed blood over both of us. I understood the extreme peril in what was happening, and fear cloaked me. Neither fight nor flight was appropriate here. Impossibly, my dystonic body lay perfectly still. Son shouted, "Get ENT up here. NOW!" He was afraid too. Now I was *really* afraid. Within what seemed like ten seconds my tiny room was filled with over a dozen people.

> *There once was a resident, Ruiz,*
> *Who was asked, "Come and help, if you please."*
> *He arrived at my room*
> *In a terrible zoom*
> *And stopped the blood's flowing with ease.*

Nurses came and changed my blood-soaked sheets.

The rest of my hospital stay was a vacation without Demerol or lead screens. Lew visited every morning, my mother spent the day, my cousin Ernie came every day after work, and my sister Evy looked after my mother and maintained a continual presence and a careful watch over me. Cards and letters appeared from nowhere and a flower garden bloomed on the windowsill. I called Judith and Daniel and confirmed to them in my own voice what my mother had already told them, "Operation finished. Feeling better. See you soon. I love you."

Two days after the seeds were removed, I was discharged. Five days later, I returned to Dr. Son for a follow up examination. The tumor had disappeared.

CHAPTER 14

Sophomore Drill, 1961–1962

At the autumn beginning of my sophomore year, I moved to one of Yale's residential colleges and set out after an even more vibrant intellectual diet. As usual during the flu season, my father gave early doses of the flu vaccine to his family. After the vaccination, my dystonia became more severe. My walking became precarious and my hands became less reliable. In short, my body became less predictable to others and less dependable to me. Was it sub-clinical encephalitis pursuant to the vaccine? Or was it coincidence? I never talked about it with my father, although I have not had any vaccinations of any sort since, and when I left the country, my physician mother oftentimes signed the documents that stated I was vaccinated from smallpox.

Again, my life was pulled out from under me. Too despondent for tears, I began to speak like a robot, the old-fashioned kind whose voice held no hint of feeling much less of distress. Robots feel no pain. I went to New York to see Cooper who had no interest in why things had deteriorated. I'd already had three operations; a fourth would be pushing it. Maybe he thought I had nothing to lose. Thus it was that I had my fourth operation in the lush operating theater that had been built in the two years since my third surgery in high school.

Again, I went through the familiar indignities. They shaved my head, shot air into the ventricles of my brain, tightened stainless steel screws down into my skull, and drilled a hole in my head. Such a shock — that sound. Then they inserted a probe into my brain vectored toward my thalamus. Again Cooper directed me to perform hand movements out of a clinical neurologist's tool kit, like touching my thumbs to my fingers. Again, I was awake throughout the whole procedure.

After a month in the hospital recuperating, I was almost back to where I had been before the flu shot. I could not write, but I did walk, if with a pronounced limp. My right arm remained bent at the elbow. As before, involuntary muscle spasms made my body changeable and caused movement and twisting as though restless. Under stress, my symptoms worsened and when I slept, my body was calm. But perhaps, most importantly, my dystonia stabilized and would not become more severe for some forty years.

I limped back to Mother Yale and she opened her arms to receive me.

Before restarting classes formally, I audited courses: Arthur and Mary Wright in Chinese history, Karl Deutsch in international relations, Henri Peyre in French literature, Vincent Scully in Greek art, Alan Anderson in mathematical logic and other courses from a palette of greatness. Sophomore year courses were even more exciting than my freshman year courses. The number of insights I made into new worlds came so rapidly I could have gotten a speeding ticket.

Yale was famous for its innovative architecture and in my junior year I moved into the newly built Morse College. For the next two years I had the pleasure of living in an architectural masterpiece designed by Eero Saarinen. Morse College featured suites for eight students, and I found myself spending much time with my suite mates, Greg, Gene, Gary, David, Joe, Tom, and Rick.

I wrestled with Greg. Although my disability interfered with my wrestling and I was ill trained, I was strong and quick and once achieved the sweet victory of a pin. Greg went on to be a hero, flying a Marine A-6 Intruder in Viet Nam.

Gene and I were close and had frequent conversations into the night. Once, we took peyote buttons together — our first psychedelic experience. From across the room I threw an apple core at Gene's eye and hit it — bingo! For me, this was an unprecedented and impossible feat of hand and eye coordination. Later in life I would also perform feats impossible to my dystonia.

Gary was soft and studious. He was deliberately but painfully separated from his beloved high school sweetheart and future wife who was at Oberlin. Later he would become a famous authority on Japan. On the side he would help save my life. Even then he had a generous and accurate concern for my interests and arranged that I see a woman at Oberlin and urged me to go on a freedom ride in the south.

Joe Lieberman slept only four hours a night and finished a biography of a Connecticut boss for his senior thesis. We all fantasized that he would be president some day. He later did run for vice-president and probably won — at least the election. He also ran in the primary for president. He is now a senator.

Tom was the most brilliant of us. Although he had never taken symbolic

logic he had an uncanny knack for solving problems. Gene and I came to
him in moments of intellectual despair.

The first time I met Rick he grabbed me by my button-down collar and
picked me up with one huge paw. He reminded me of brother Bear who was
always saying, "I'm gonna knock your head clean off."

Off to one side of the group was David, who later became a writer and
filmmaker. During our years at Yale and even after, as our group dynamics,
relationships and interactions underwent changes, I fantasized that David
might make a film about us.

Once a week my mother came to clean my room; I would know she had
been there by my orderly surroundings and a slight drop in the level of
my rum flask, the only spirit except holiday wine I ever knew her to drink.
Once a week I would know my Uncle Rudi had been there because on my
desk I would find a perfect pastrami sandwich from Chuck's Delicatessen.
Although proud that I went to Yale, Uncle Rudi was sure they didn't feed me
right.

During that year, I also started an exciting special major in politics and
economics cooked up by Charles E. Lindblom in which two teachers taught
classes of ten and where we read a book a week and wrote a paper on it. I
wrote by dictation to his secretary, Miss Granger, a strategy that I use to this
day. I also devised other disability strategies like asking a fellow student with
good handwriting to make a carbon copy of his lecture notes.

I was not only an excellent student in my courses but an astute observer
of myself. I asked one of my parents' psychoanalyst friends, Clair Selzer, to
recommend a shrink, and soon I was seeing Albert Solnit at the Yale Child
Studies Center. Since I had no one to compare him to, I did not then realize that he was a master. The first time I told the story of my disability, it was
to Solnit and I cried. The second time I told the story, it was to my friends
at Morse College. I cried, but it was easier. The third time I told the story,
it was in my senior year in front of my senior society, which functioned partially as an encounter group before such groups became fad. I did not cry. By
the end of college I had pretty much come to terms with the psychological
aspects of my disability. It would not be until many years later when I worked
for the Carnegie Council on Children that I would come to terms with the
social and political aspects of my disability.

After seeing Solnit for several months, I asked him to refer me to a neurologist. He referred me to Lewis Levy. Levy and I talked. This move was a
declaration of medical independence from my father who was also my physician. Never again would I be forced to rely on my father for matters medical,
although usually I would. As it turned out, Levy was the same neurologist,

friend and colleague my father had consulted about my disability when I was eight, and probably the one who referred me to Denny-Brown.

On the weekends, when my friends went to mixers, I went home. I had no conception of how to spend time with women and was afraid to find out. I later turned this into a virtue by inviting my classmates to my house after football games or to my mother's table on Saturday evenings. To each of these dinners I invited a different professor and a different group of friends. My mother savored these gatherings immensely. She enjoyed preparing the meals, and she relished charming my fellow students in a way that she never would have dreamt of doing with my sister's boyfriends.

During junior year, I invited Allan Bloom, the well-known academic, to my parents' house for dinner. My invitation to him was natural. On a year's leave from Cornell to teach at Yale, Bloom lived in a residential dorm and did not appear happy. I later read that Cornell was an agonizing experience for him. Allan chain smoked strong French cigarettes and as he lit the first one, my father, hardly without his faults, lit into Bloom with the delicacy of a righteous thug. "You know, Professor Bloom, it has been my professional experience as a physician that smoking can kill you."

"All life ends with death," Bloom replied. Perhaps Bloom believed that he was engaged in Socratic dialogue. But my father's life had never allowed him the luxury of Socratic speech. By the time my mother served an exquisite apple strudel, Allan was literally unable to speak. On the way out the door, he was a pathetic figure, fumbling and babbling in tongues.

CHAPTER 15

Slow Burn, April 1988

Although it was a definite possibility that the radiation seeds might indeed have cured my cancer, the chances of the little bastard having sent micro metastatic messengers elsewhere, particularly to the lymph nodes in my neck, was too great to stop treatment. A six-megavolt linear accelerator would now channel high-energy radiation through two portals on either side of my neck and jaw.

The eccentric movements of my dystonia concerned me. In the hospital, with blood choking my throat, I had been able to lie perfectly still. In the tear gas of graduate school, I had been able to scurry quickly. Somehow, in these dangerous situations, I had been able to "break out" of my disability. But now, with six megavolts hurling photons at me, I knew I was bound to move. Movement would distort the effectiveness of the radiation in unexpected ways. Further, if I moved certain organs into the beam, it would create unacceptable risks. As my radiation treatments would continue for five weeks, and as my life was at issue, the situation was serious.

I consulted Lew who spoke of anesthetics with a short half-life, which we left as a last resort because they would require an I.V. and a physician. Fortunately, our solution of first resort worked: a combination of breathing techniques and relaxation exercises combined with massive doses of the relaxing oral benzodiazepines which in lower dose are a standard medical treatment for dystonia.

I am a good patient, not in the sense of passivity, but rather in the sense of appropriate active collaboration. This is partly because I grew up in a family of physicians; partly because I have a disability, which gives me a too long experience with the medical world; partly because of my own good sense; partly because I was willing to do the necessary research even before the Internet; and partly because of Lew's training. Lew offered me a non-traditional model of consultation and advice. Unlike most other doctors who keep their own counsel, reach a decision and then tell you what to do, at every stage

Lew asked me what I thought and framed my ignorance with his knowledge. This approach suited me perfectly, and I put Lew's training into practice in my conversations with other physicians, which seemed to suit them too.

For the next five weeks I awoke every morning at seven thirty, swallowed benzodiazepines as part of my breakfast, staggered sedated to the car where my mother waited to drive me to the Yale–New Haven Hospital for my radiation treatments. As the days passed, I discovered that my body behaved yet better if I wound a rope around both my feet to help keep myself still. Then a zip on one side, a zap on the other, stagger back to the car and then up the steps of my mother's house, and then to sleep for three or four hours.

During those weeks in New Haven, with certain modifications, I led a variation of the lifeless life that I had led during the worst of my adolescent disability. On weekends, I took the bus back to Albany and reveled in Daniel's company. Week by week, I could actually see Daniel growing up. By the time I returned home six weeks later, he had grown in years. Not only did he act more mature, but his syntax was more complex, his taste in movies changed from kid films to Woody Allen and Francis Ford Coppola.

Surely my death would be a blow to him but not the crushing one that it would have been only six weeks before. Daniel's leaps of growth notwithstanding, as each Sunday drew to a close, it pained me to leave him.

During that time, I became aware of the emerging and disgusting growth industry in dying. Bernard Siegal, M.D., is a pioneer in this industry. Since New Haven is Siegal's base, it was natural that I contacted Exceptional Cancer Patients or ECAP, which is Siegal's business. It was fortunate that I did so. The woman who interviewed me had cancer, as did everyone in the group.

People with cancer have much to say to other people with cancer. Indeed, people with cancer have much to say to other people. For all of its murderous intent, cancer can lead to exquisite wisdom. Siegal had observed this long before me. I attended the ECAP group once a week and profited immensely. This was, however, despite my substantial theoretical disagreements. While I am open to Bernie Siegal's claims borrowed from the Simentons that cancer has a direct psychological cause, there is nothing in my reading or experience that proves this to be true. As a Ph.D., I well know the difference between coincidence, correlation and causality.

What I found most objectionable was the Peter Pan technique of visualization: think hard enough and you can fly. And while, as Solnit had insisted, optimism has a place with cancer, except in the case of artists, dreamers, and tyrants, those parts of life that can be substantially influenced by imagination are reasonably narrow. I also disliked the unsavory subtext: if you don't get well, you didn't visualize hard enough, you didn't believe deeply enough, you didn't think the right thoughts ... you didn't ... you didn't ... which essentially leaves the cancer patient in a Catch-22 game that cannot be won. It is not only my Judaism that makes Christian Science unpalatable; it is also my science. I did, however, totally agree with Siegal about taking responsibility for one's own body and taking charge of one's own care. Indeed, my own position was more radical as I partially reverted to an adolescent existentialism, a combination of comic book superheroes and Sartre.

My weekly participation in Siegal's New Haven group was a highlight during a time of tedium. Later in Albany, I continued to belong to a cancer group for the direct help it gave me as well as the indirect help that came by way of helping others, but ultimately because I found there people who shared my intimacy with death and, with me, insisted on life.

As the weeks progressed, swallowing my food became more painful and I lost significant weight even though I swallowed viscous Novocain as a first course to each radiation treatment. In the last week of radiation treatment, the skin fried off the front of my neck. I was alarmed; Son had expected it. The treatments continued. As I soaked my throat in saline and coated it with Vaseline, I mused over the curious combination of late twentieth-century high-voltage radiation therapy and nineteenth-century antiseptic first aid nursing.

My saliva first thickened and then diminished. Never before had I justly reckoned the value of spit. Spit made swallowing easier, chewing more enjoyable and speaking easier. To this day, I miss my spit. This lack of spit was an impairment around which a new aspect of disability was constructed. I eased this problem by chewing four pieces of sugarless bubblegum at a time, a practice that I developed on my own and continue to this day.

The gum provided me with a bit of comic relief in the middle of my cancer therapy when I went to the grocery store to purchase some bubblegum for the dry mouth caused by the radiation. A group of half a dozen kids had probably watched me make the purchase through the window of the neighborhood grocery store. As I hobbled home, one of the kids grabbed my wallet from my pocket, which sparked a remarkable exchange. The gang broke into two factions, one of which argued that I should be treated differently because of my disability, the second arguing that I should be treated like anyone else.

In theory, I agreed with the second group and although I truly wanted my wallet back, I was also fascinated by the discussion. The first faction lost, and I lost my wallet. Of course, I was richer and whiter, but I regarded the theft not so much as a redistribution of wealth but as a personal violation. I was reduced to a pathetic plea, "Keep the money, but throw my wallet into the trash can on the corner."

Apparently the kids found that request reasonable because I found the empty wallet in the garbage can. And this left me with further questions: Would they have left the wallet had I not been disabled? Would they have harmed me had I not been disabled? *I will never know.* My life as a disabled person is filled with such questions.

Muggings and the general perplexities of life notwithstanding, radiation continued leaving me tired, depressed or both. Whatever I was, I was clear: the only way to fulfill my responsibility to live was to be monomaniacal about my recovery. Intimate talks with close friends, bonding again with my mother, long and long-distance telephone conversations, cable TV, naps, the rediscovery of New Haven — all helped ease the tedium of those weeks of treatment.

As those who are familiar with the area know, Yale had become New Haven's only industry. And downtown New Haven, a pioneer in '50s style urban renewal, was a disaster. Credit to me then that while I was in New Haven, I found a jewel amidst the junk: Macy's downtown bargain basement. Twice a week, I went to Macy's to buy clothes, some as presents, but more for myself. I bought pants, shirts, jackets and socks, fully aware that I was buying them as a kind of life insurance. New socks are for the living. And, prudent man that I am, I guaranteed my future at bargain basement prices. One day while admiring one of my purchases, I recalled my father's pleasure at his half-price Anderson Little suits and smiled. I am not my father's son for nothing.

Three weeks into my radiation, my friend Gary Saxonhouse flew in for the afternoon. I cried tears of relief and love. We spent an afternoon whose simple details became the stuff of lifelong memories. In European fashion, Yale is packed with intimate grassy courtyards. The Newman Center where we sat and talked was filled with an artful garden of flowering shrubs in full spring blossom.

As he left, Gary and I hugged, and I said, "I love you."

I had missed so many opportunities to express my love. I would miss no more.

CHAPTER 16

Biting the Big Apple,
1963–1964

Since my decision to go to Hopkins in sixth grade, I had been as distant from women as one galaxy from another. In order to get to know women and to get a little distance from home, towards the end of sophomore year I applied for transfer to co-educational schools. Harvard and Swarthmore both accepted me, but when I found out that graduation would take four years, versus Yale's three, I decided to stay put.

At school when a woman was at a table, I chose another. I ignored my sister and her friends, especially those who, had I not been disabled, should have attracted me. I knew that something was missing and knew that it involved half the people in the world. To solve this dilemma, I devised a quaint little motto: GO OUT. MAKE OUT. MAKE IT. I believed that if only I followed this elegant and simple progression in language my sexuality would blossom.

In my junior year, Gary fixed me up with Chris, a beautiful and soft-spoken harpist at Oberlin where music seemed to drift out of every window. It was a very simple weekend, really. Chris and I went for a walk and studied. I fell in love with her. I did not know such things could build in only a weekend. I was too ignorant even to write her, let alone go back for another visit.

What had gone wrong? I did not have the tools to think, much less act. Love had moved out of the family circle and into the larger world and at the same time assumed an erotic component. Now, knowing sex was a prerequisite to knowing love. And knowing both were prerequisites to growing up. I had no experience. None.

This lack of experience was one of the harshest penalties of having a disability. Many able-bodied people have years to learn: the disabled, at least in my case, learn virtually nothing.

I tried again. My sister fixed me up with Audrey. We met in New York at Cinema I and watched a foreign film I don't remember because I was occupied with the problem of how to touch Audrey. Where do you touch a woman? On the arm? Perhaps a leg? Maybe you put your arm around her shoulder? Or do you try to hold her hand? But that would be too dangerous; she might not hold yours. Perhaps a breast? What about a pat on the head? Or a tweak of the ear lobe — did Audrey have ear lobes? Or a light caress on the nose? I had no idea. I settled for a grip on her closest shoulder. Audrey concentrated on the film. So there we were in Cinema I, Audrey watching, me clutching, afraid to let go. The end of the movie was a welcome relief to both of us.

My physics teacher, Professor Beringer, had said, "When force doesn't work, you're not using enough." My disability had taught me that it was often best to tackle the hardest obstacles first. As I had failed utterly to MAKE OUT, I now reformulated my elegant theory. I would reverse the order: MAKE IT. MAKE OUT. GO OUT.

If I did the hardest thing first, everything else would be child's play!

But how best to MAKE IT? In those days, there were no women at Yale, which was partly why I chose it in the first place. There were my sister's friends, but I was not on speaking terms with them. Every route seemed a dead end, and I had no cognitive map.

Then a plan began to develop. Gene, Greg and I would drive to New York; find a prostitute and MAKE IT. Although we each had our individual, pressing reasons, it would be a group effort.

We left New Haven one Friday evening in my Uncle Egon's 310 horsepower, fuel-injected, two-tone Oldsmobile compact. Greg drove because my unpredictable muscle contractions make it impossible for me to drive safely. I took my accustomed place in the suicide seat. Gene stretched out in the back seat. The jet-propelled hockey puck, as Gene liked to call it, averaged ninety miles an hour on its journey into New York. We did not get a speeding ticket.

We knew about as much about Manhattan as teenagers from Long Island.

Foreigners in New York City looking for a prostitute, we cruised down Broadway. The number of people was staggering. The Olds went slowly. Traffic ran by on our sides and nudged us from the rear. I knew nothing about male prostitution or child porn or runaways or about the life expectancy or upper age limits of the profession. Thus was I out on the prowl with the rudimentary idea that four million New Yorkers were possible prostitutes.

Though Gene's knowledge of the social world was far more extensive than mine, he didn't know how to identify a prostitute either. I tried to say something that would not embarrass us. "Which way should we turn?" seemed safe.

Farther down Broadway became the Great White Way. Forty-second

Street was dazzling, with movie marquee after movie marquee. Throngs, masses, hordes of people marched up and down the streets, crossing over and back, going in and out of movies and shops.

"Too many people," Greg said.

"Isn't it amazing that they don't bump into each other?" I said.

"Too many people for whores, I meant," Greg said, and he accelerated toward 34th Street.

"Let's go down to the Village," Gene directed.

The Village was not as crowded as midtown. And, unlike the garment district, there were women. Definitely a place of promise. Greg shifted from prowl to cruise. Most of the women were with men. Then we saw a lone woman walking down Bleecker Street. "This is it," Greg said. We followed her for a short distance, waiting for a sign. Her hand went into her purse. Perhaps this was a sign, an advertisement. She stopped abruptly and looked behind her. Her eyes stopped on the Oldsmobile. Greg was right; this was it. Then she turned around, inserted keys into a door and disappeared.

By now the problem of how to approach a prostitute was academic. We simply couldn't find one. We headed downtown past Houston Street, through the empty loft buildings of SoHo, through Little Italy and Chinatown. We ended up at the South Street Seaport and saw the Brooklyn Bridge.

It was two o'clock in the morning as we headed up Park Avenue toward 125th Street. Here in Harlem, our social maps were even less adequate. The streets were bare and the Apollo was closed; even the bars were closed.

Greg hung a left off 125th and went south down Lenox. The avenue was almost empty. Like the garment district after working hours, this was Lenox asleep. A young, black woman in a fly-front trench coat was leaning against a doorway at 116th Street. She was reading. She looked up as we passed. Greg stopped the car.

"This is the place," he said.

"What place?" I asked.

"Back there, that woman," Greg answered.

"That woman must be out there for some reason," Gene said.

By now we surely had eliminated every other possibility in the city.

We got out of the car and walked over to her.

"Hello," she said,

"Hello," Greg said.

She was reading *The Fall* by Albert Camus. I had just read it for a French literature course.

Heart leaping, I took an existential leap. "How do you like the book?" I asked.

"Compelling," the woman answered. "What do you boys want?"

It was true, of course. The book *was* compelling and we *were* boys.

"Do you want to come upstairs? We have a kind of club."

She led. Greg followed. Gene next. Me last. My legs were shaking, not the tremor characteristic of my dystonia but a new kind of weak shake that started in my stomach.

"Baby, you're scared," I thought.

It was one long flight until she opened a door and we all walked into a large, dim room painted pea green. There was a small bar along one wall. "This is the palace, boys," she laughed. "It's late. All the other girls have gone home."

An old man was tending bar. "We got bourbon, rye, and Bud. Sit down and make yourselves at home." On a small radio, James Brown sang softly. "Yep, would have been a clean sweep for New York. Yankees won. Dodgers won. Giants won." Greg and Gene had Buds. I asked the man for a double bourbon. He looked at me and laughed. "You sure ready for a party!"

The woman sat at the bar. "Can I have some ginger ale, Fred?" She quickly finished it and slowly turned to us. "You get thirsty standing down there under the moon."

"At least it ain't summer," Fred said, and he laughed again.

It was not my fantasy palace with crimson drapes, Victorian coat rack and high-fidelity sound system, but it was a warm, friendly place.

"I'm in no hurry. I sleep late Saturdays. My name is Diana."

We introduced ourselves.

"How do you want to do this?" Diana asked.

Gene and I were silent. Greg said, "I'll go first."

"All right, come right along." Diana put down her glass and she and Greg walked to a door at the back of the room. Diana opened it. She and Greg went in. The door closed.

I picked up the glass of bourbon. The shakiness spread from my stomach, through my pounding heart, and into my arms and hands, which trembled around the glass, and mingled with the tremor of my disability. My eyes were getting used to the dim light. There were four doors off the room, two at either end. I guessed that must be where other women conducted their business at more reasonable hours.

I had no concept of what the business involved. What would I do when it was my turn? The question had no answer. I pushed it away to the back of my brain and put a padlock on it.

Doubtless Gene was thinking his own thoughts. We were alone, together. I asked Fred for another bourbon.

"Single or double?"

"Double." I entered a glazed hibernation, a meditation, a nothingness that has left no memories. I don't know how much time passed, but Greg came out of the door and sat down at the bar.

"Who's next?" he asked, looking at Gene and me. I was no more ready than I had been when we first came upstairs.

"Why don't you go?" I said to Gene, trying to make it sound like a gracious offer.

Gene got up. He walked over to the open door. It closed behind him.

Greg was talkative and radiated contentment. He had accomplished what he came to do. Driving to New York, around New York for seven hours, then ending up at ll6th Street and Lenox Avenue and making it with a prostitute. It was all an enjoyable excursion. Now he was ready to savor it.

He asked Fred for another Bud. Greg made some joke at which Fred laughed and returned another one. Laughter had left my repertory, never mind joking. I asked Fred for another double bourbon. Greg leaned over to me and said something about it not being a good idea to drink too much at such times. I followed his advice and sipped slowly. I returned to my state of suspension. Greg and Fred bantered in the distance. Again, I have no recollection of how long it was before Gene came out of the room and sat at the bar.

Gene asked for a Bud, and I swallowed the last of my bourbon. I slid off my stool and walked endless steps to the open door. Diana closed it behind me. She had on a red satin robe. The room was small and the same pea green color as the big room. There was a small dresser on one wall, coat hooks on the other, and a sink in the corner. Along the wall opposite the door was a bed. Diana walked over to the bed and sat down.

I stood still near the closed door. Diana looked at me. "Why don't you come sit here?" she asked, patting the bed. "I want to talk with you."

I walked over and sat on the bed. "I want to talk, too," I said in a voice that was not yet my own.

"This is your first time, isn't it?"

"Yes."

"Don't worry. We'll take it nice and easy." Diana put her hand on mine. "I won't rush you or anything. Tell me what you like to do."

"Read, for one."

"Me, too."

"I noticed." The voice was becoming my own.

"It gets me out of this strange life into something that makes sense."

I looked up at her. "That's why I'm here."

"How do you mean?"

"I mean, there are things, too many, not in my life. I don't know about so much, too much. That's why I'm here," I repeated.

"So you come to Lenox Avenue and I read." We both laughed.

"You got a handicap."

"Yes," I said.

"Is that why it's your first time?"

I had to think about it. "I don't know. Probably."

"Is there anything special you can't do?" Diana asked.

"I don't know."

"Is there anything special you want me to do?" Diana asked.

"Please go easy."

"You want to take your clothes off?" She laughed. "You make yourself at home."

"Sure," I said and got undressed.

Meanwhile back at Yale, Ed Lindblom, the director of my program in politics and economics, left for India to be economic advisor to the ambassador, Chester Bowles. This caused me to drop out of my major for my senior year and create my own major of politics, economics and mathematics. This essentially meant that I took only graduate courses taught by the best professors at Yale.

When I presented myself along with some fifty graduate students at Richard Bernstein's first class in a course on Wittgenstein, Bernstein threw up his hands and said, "There are far too many students here for a respectable seminar. Will all first year students please leave?" As I was not a first year graduate student, I took him at his word and stayed in my seat. Bernstein continued to pare down the class using other categories that did not apply to undergraduate me. Eventually there were sufficiently few students left so as to satisfy Bernstein, who recognized all with the exception of one. He turned to me and asked who I was and what I was doing there. To my technically true answers, he replied, "You are obnoxiously persistent so I welcome you to this course."

My course on formal modal logic and law at the Yale Law School left me horrified. As one who had no concept of a career of my own, the narrowness and premature careerism of the law students was shocking and alien to me. I also took Harold Lasswell's course on personality and politics. Here again I admired the professor but regarded the students with contempt for mechanically applying his theories of personality and aping the master rather than learning from him.

At the end of my time at Yale in 1964, I took a seminar on modern architecture with Vincent Scully, a man of drama and dash. It was the year of the New York World's Fair and we traveled there in a VW bus. We hopped around from building to building, Scully offering and eliciting comment on each. Several hours later we arrived at Philip Johnson's New York State pavilion. Scully walked back and forth through the space that the structure defined, walked over to a public phone, called Johnson and said, "It's a masterpiece!"

I could have said the same about my Yale education, a combination of world's fair and absolute masterpiece — and a fabulous place to grow up. Given the time I lost to surgery, I graduated in three years instead of four — *magna cum laude*.

Mind honed, eyes opened, body initiated and forever changed, I left Yale with the echo of Martin Luther King's commencement address propelling me into the dream of the great world beyond.

CHAPTER 17

What, Me Worry?
Spring 1988

All in all, I was radiant and as part of my post-radiation follow-up, Steven Parnes M.D., the head of Albany's ENT Department, was giving me his usual eagle-eyed examination. His hands flew over the inside of my mouth, the base of my tongue, over the cervical nodes. I was just about to sign off with my customary "N.E.D.?"—no evidence of disease—when I asked him to examine the nodes at the back of my neck.

Was I paranoid, fearful or alert? I could never be sure. Parnes palpated the nodes. He lingered at the intersection of an imaginary line going downward through my ear and another line drawn backward through my jaw. The lines felt real to me. He pushed and pushed again. He did not like what he felt. "There's a bump there that might be cancer," he said. "I'm going to schedule you for a CAT scan as soon as possible."

I was furious. Why a CAT scan? The last thing I wanted practiced on me was a defensive medicine that substitutes technology for proficiency. Aside from being expensive, defensive medicine tends to reveal not the probable but the possible. I had enough real things to go through already. I did not express my fury to Parnes, but I did express my anger to Rick as he drove me to my office at the university. As we climbed the stairs to my third floor office, I felt myself turning from Bruce Wayne into Batman, shifting gears from rest to alertness, from fatigue to activity, from one person to two people. I grasped the banister extra firmly, partly in anger and partly because of my disability, and said, "I'm going to call Son."

Within a minute I had Son on the phone and I was asking him my usual, "How are you?" This combination of bad joke and question never failed to get his attention. "Busy day," he answered in the Korean accent that was by now thoroughly familiar to me. "How are you doing?"

"I don't know. That's what I wanted to ask you. The ENT man here felt something in my neck. He wants to do a CAT scan."

"Where is the lump?" asked Son. I described where it was. "Have the CAT scan done and bring it down here," Son said. "What you're describing is consistent with trauma from the inserts. Just bring the CAT scan down. Don't worry."

Me worry? What is worry when compared to dread? To confuse rational fear with anxiety can be deadly. I was not a hypochondriac full of irrational anxiety, but rather an ill man full of genuine, honest alertness and it was dangerous for me to be anything but flawless in my response to symptoms.

I had the CAT scan done in Albany, then made the trip to New Haven to see Son. In the examining room, Son scanned the sections and quickly came upon the lump that Parnes had noticed in Albany. "I don't think there is much reason to worry," he said. "What I see in the CAT scan is consistent with the effects of the procedure that we did on you."

But like N.E.D., "consistent" is another medical expression that hedges its bets. In my case, Son's interpretation of the CAT scan as "consistent with the procedure" did not contradict an interpretation that found it consistent with cancer. Consistent did not mean "caused by." Lew Levy had once told me that medicine was more an art than a science. In some measure medical diagnosis is the art of judging likelihoods. At some point in such judgments, a further test may be called for. The results of this test, in turn, have to be judged. I was interested in only one question: cancer or no? But that's not the way medicine works.

"If you don't mind sitting around," Son said, "I'd like to take you to the head and neck seminar at four this afternoon." The head and neck seminar was Yale's interdisciplinary team of ENT people, therapeutic radiation people, oncologists, plastic surgeons, et cetera who met to discuss issues regarding head and neck cancer. It was located at the back of the suite of offices where I had gone to see Sasaki. My mother, Rick and I followed the signs through the passageways of the Yale–New Haven Hospital to a back room in Sasaki's office suite. Dr. Son opened the door and invited me in. My mother and Rick were not invited to this party. The door closed. It was evident to me that my case had been discussed beforehand. One by one the members of the Yale Head and Neck Cancer Seminar examined me. At the end of this, they excused me from the room, a child banished from an adult party. Sasaki said that I would be hearing from him.

Feeling victorious, Rick and I drove back to Albany. Surely, if I had not been cleared, they would have asked me to stick around. We celebrated with an animated discussion of world politics.

Three days later, my surgeon's secretary called. Sasaki wanted to see me. My confidence melted into fear. I was on a roller coaster. With the report of one physician I was terrified. With the report of another I was relieved. And while the roller coaster did not bother me — I relied on my "case mode shift" to cope with it — it did distress my friends and family, especially my mother.

Once again I divided myself in two and, CAT scan in hand, hopped a bus to New Haven. At Sasaki's office, his fingers quickly came to rest on the node in question. He glanced at the CAT scan. He was feeling the same node that was showing up on the CAT scan. He said, "Come into the other room. I'm going to do a needle biopsy." I went into a nearby room to lay down under bright lights. He gave me a local anesthetic. I lay perfectly still which, of course, is usually impossible with my dystonia. His fingers were on the gland, but when my neck tensed, the gland disappeared. He smiled and said, "Trying to hide?" He found the gland again and filled the syringe with material from it. He went back to the gland. "We're making two passes," he said.

If the results were negative, it could mean either that there was no cancer or that the needle had bypassed the malignancy. A negative finding on a needle biopsy was consistent with either. Should the first reading be negative, I would undergo a second needle biopsy. Again, the results of this second biopsy could be consistent with the absence of cancer or with the needle having missed the malignancy. Nevertheless, the odds at this point would lean to the probability of no malignancy.

The patient who looks for God-like certainty in a physician is a set-up for disappointment and anger. I was comfortable with medical judgments made on the odds by people whom I respected and whose judgments in the end were not scientific but skillful, wise, and based on clinical experience.

"What if the findings are positive?" I asked Sasaki. My mother cringed at my question. Her position was let well enough alone. Why behave like a masochist?

Why indeed? I expected the results of the biopsy to be negative. But if they were positive, I wanted to be prepared to deal with the consequences and didn't know how much time I'd have. I had to set the apparatus in place for making decisions now.

In this case, the consequence was an altogether barbaric piece of surgery called a radical neck dissection. At Yale's medical library I did a survey of surgery texts and photocopied some basic cookbook descriptions of radical neck dissections. A radical neck dissection would chop out my mastoid muscles, my exterior jugular vein, a nerve to the trapezius muscle in my back — the muscle we would use to fly if we were angels — until finally, the dissection would reveal the lymph glands underneath. These would be removed. It occurred to me that Doctor Guillotine's invention for efficient beheading was a device for the most thorough head and neck surgery.

Such a curious thing this was: to participate in the destruction of my own body to enhance the probabilities of life. No matter that a surgery is disabling, disfiguring, uncomfortable, or even life threatening. The ultimate question — life or death, being or not being — renders all other questions trivial. For me, this urgent life or death question was a major difference between having cancer and having my disability. I lived with this question every breath of every day and found strength in the image of cancer therapy as a battle, and of myself as a warrior practicing courage one skirmish at a time. I was not fighting against some new disability; I was fighting for my life.

A short while later, I was at Lew's office explaining to him what happened. I waved my articles over his desk and said, "Look what I found at the library. How to do a radical neck in one easy page!"

Lew snorted, "Surgeon talk, and textbook at that. You can't tell what the effects of taking out your mastoid muscles would be with your dystonia. You might find that if we take out the right one your neck would turn to the left. And what about your trapezius? You might have to live your life with your left arm weak. I'll tell you now; I don't like it. If the findings are positive, get in touch with me right away. I'll have to make myself smart about the alternatives."

It was a split decision. If the findings were positive, Sasaki, my surgeon, wanted to do a radical neck dissection, which Levy, my medical neurologist, did not want. Decisions on surgery are frequently matters of judgment best decided by more than one person. My father had passed on to me this article of faith: when contemplating a surgical procedure, always get a second opinion — from a medical person.

The next afternoon Sasaki called to report there were no cells in the first sample. Could I come in the next morning for a repeat? The second time around I was drugged in what now was the standard fashion. My nodes did not hide. Just to make sure, Sasaki made three passes and seemed confident that he had done a thorough job. I went back to my mother's house to await the results. Again I made the usual calls and watched my mother's then state-of-the-art cable television.

The next day Sasaki called and said, "I called pathology. There are cancer cells."

The roller coaster plunged. A passenger screamed. Without missing a beat, I asked, "What do you want to do?"

"A radical neck dissection," he said. "I can squeeze you in two weeks from today."

The bright spot on my horizon evaporated. The surgery would blow my scheduled visit with Daniel at camp.

That afternoon I returned to Lew's office and said, "I want a second opinion."

"Do you have anybody in mind?"

"Yes. Dave Fisher. What do you think of him?"

Lew answered, "Tops."

David Fisher had been a friend of my father's and was also a friend of my mother's. In fact, it was she who had advised to call him the month before. Now I had Lew's recommendation as well. Lew called Fisher from his office and arranged for me to see him at four o'clock that afternoon after his office hours.

"Give me a call when you're done?" asked Lew.

"Sure." I said and left.

My mother waited with me while Dr. Fisher took a brief history; I did the talking with no extra questions required. I gave him a list of the possible causes for the cancer, the dates, the staging, the radiation therapy, et cetera. Fisher placed a call to the Yale Pathology Department and tracked down the pathologist who had read my slides. The pathologist had no doubts. It was cancer. Fisher repeated this to my mother and me. He then added a crucial missing link. The pathologist who read the slides was one of Yale's best. I pressed the point, "Are you completely comfortable in relying on him and his judgment?"

"Yes, I am. He's absolutely top-flight."

I started to ask a question when Fisher broke in, "Before we talk any more, I would like to examine you." He took me into an examination room and quickly found the offending node. Then he did part of a normal physical. He asked me some nostalgic pre-cancer questions that triggered in me a pathetic longing to see Roberta Flesh, my primary care physician, for some innocent pre-cancer illness. I was now in the hands of specialists and superspecialists and this was my first encounter with a medical oncologist.

The difference in Fisher's exam was the ancient and honorable difference between medical person and surgeon. When the history and exam were complete, Fisher wrote down a thorough set of notes. Later he would send his opinion to Sasaki and Levy. Thus far, I had spent some forty-five minutes in Fisher's office, a long time for a history and an exam. Like Lew and my father, Fisher was from the old school, patience with patients. Given the choice between competence and care, I choose competence every time. Nevertheless, care and concern are important; if nothing else they prompt competence.

My questions to Fisher were relevant and on target and he answered all of them. His answers provided information that later on would enable me to ask questions that would make contributions to my own treatment plan.

We returned to Fisher's consultation room for what he may have envisaged as a brief discussion. I wanted to go through the logic of my illness. I wanted to dissect layer after layer of fact and possibilities. After about ten minutes I think Fisher quite enjoyed the discussion. After about two hours, I knew much more about my cancer and about cancer in general. I was set to do some more reading. My mother stayed with me throughout all this time and, though hardly disinterested, she kept her physician's cool.

I remain grateful to Fisher for those two hours. I learned much, tested what I knew, learned what to ask, and how to ask it. Consultation rooms and time spent with patients are casualties of modern medical bureaucracy. Fisher, a clinical professor at Yale, had on his wall a teaching award like the one my father had on his wall years ago. He was an excellent teacher. I was an excellent student.

Since my dystonia made the outcomes of a radical neck dissection more uncertain, over the next several days, Fisher, Sasaki, Levy and I discussed the possible debilitating side effects and potentially greater impact on quality of life. When it came to disability, I was the expert. Although I often do not like my disability, I have learned to live with it, and I am not afraid of it. I know it is not the end. Of course, further disability would be an unwelcome unknown. However, life itself is almost always the first priority. In this I find myself in unexpected agreement with the cancer surgeon.

Others without my experience of disability might feel differently. That a person is better off dead is facile. Few people would be better off dead, though death is always an option. I knew how to take my own life and was willing to contemplate situations where I might choose to do so. But it would take more than having my head always pointed to my left side. Although the radical dissection might be more disabling for me, I made sure that Lew realized that I did not mind increased disability as much as I minded death. When I shared some of this with Lew, he said, "We'll do whatever we have to do to keep you alive, but I'm not prepared to see you give up."

The next afternoon I received three phone calls. The first was from Sasaki who told me he would do a functional neck dissection followed by chemotherapy. I asked, "Does it offer the same odds of killing the cancer as the radical neck dissection?"

"I can't tell about the odds, but a functional neck dissection with chemotherapy is a medically prudent alternative."

"After I talk with Lew and Dr. Fisher I'll get back to you."

"There's no hurry. Dr. Levy and Dr. Fisher are in favor of the functional dissection. I can plan later on."

The second call was from Lew who expressed pleasure that the partial dissection would leave my mastoid muscles intact and would spare the nerves to the trapezius. My disability would be held at bay.

The third call was from Fisher who reported that he had opted for a functional on Lew's advice. When I asked him, "Which do you think has the most likelihood of saving my life?" he replied, "I can't really tell. My hunch is they're about the same." I asked him about the chemotherapy. "The University of Pittsburgh has done some research on Methotrexate 5-FU with Leucovorin recovery. I did some checking and the evidence shows even more promise than the published results."

Before we hung up I thanked Fisher for his invaluable intervention. Years later, I would learn that Fisher had made an even more valuable intervention when my surgeons and doctors concluded that I should be spared any further aggressive intervention and be left to die in peace. But Fisher protested, "Bill wants to fight. If he wants to fight, we should help him."

Had I not been disabled, would the inclination to "make things easy" for Bill still have existed? Just one more thing I'll never know.

The next day I went to the Yale Medical Library to track down two different strands. One was neck dissection. The second was chemotherapy. While there was a little on each of these, there was no material on functional neck dissection coupled with chemotherapy. I found enough articles on neck dissections to realize they were a demanding procedure whether it was a modified functional or a radical. Most studies cited a mortality rate of around one percent. In Sasaki's hands, I cut that in half—trivial compared with my odds of getting winged by the cancer. Surgical techniques, the handling of the flaps, the suction under the flaps, et cetera, all had improved in the last decade. Surgery was more difficult although not totally compromised in an irradiated field, such as my neck was.

In a book on head and neck surgery, I came across two finely illustrated and meticulously written chapters by Sasaki, one on functional dissections, the other on radical dissections. Although the functional dissection seemed a more difficult procedure, it appealed to me because of its elegance and because it spared many of the vital conduits that pass through the neck and would not disturb my neurology. It reminded me less of the Guillotine. Nonetheless, I could not afford to be seduced by elegance. The main drawback was that the surgeon could not be sure of having got all the lymph nodes.

The radical, in principle, seemed like an altogether simple operation. Essentially, it was one chop toward the base of the neck, one chop toward the top of the neck, and tear out the tissue in between. Of course, functional or radical, each layer had to be delicately exposed, and there were nerves and arteries that could not be sacrificed. Each procedure was truly a dissection, exposing first one layer of anatomy, dealing with it, and then proceeding to the layer of anatomy that it covered.

I copied all the relevant articles on neck dissection and then started my research on head and neck chemotherapy. Disappointed, I discovered that clinical oncology was not exactly a science. Most of the literature on chemotherapy was about what worked for what, more clinical documentation than true scientific research.

I was soon disabused of a common prejudice about chemotherapy — that chemotherapy is used when everything else has failed, that only rarely does it actually cure and more often, it just palliates or leads to remission. There are cases where chemotherapy not only works but also cures. Chemotherapy is not merely an agonizing prolongation of life. In many cases it makes life more pleasant, and sometimes by itself or in conjunction with other therapies, it cures. I also learned about such things as the law of kinetics which holds that chemotherapy cuts the number of cancer cells in half, that number in half, et cetera. Thus, the most dramatic effect occurs at the beginning. Towards the end, presumably my own immune system would take over.

Late that afternoon, I walked out of the comfortably air-conditioned Yale Medical Library into soggy heat with photocopies of many articles. The articles essentially agreed on two points: If you were going to die, chances were pretty good that you would meet your murderer in the first two years. Second, there could be a distant metastasis, loss of local control, or loss of regional control. With any one of these, the cancer would have won. I needed control of all three. Surgery to the glands in my neck would only affect the regional control of my neck, leaving open the possibility of distant metastasis, pretty uniformly fatal, or a lapse in local control of the original tumor.

I had already lost regional control. There were only a few studies that dealt with the outcome of people with regional control failure. Was this because we were a small group? Or was it, as Gary pointed out, because contingent probabilities had not yet entered the statistical analyses of the studies? Other possibilities I had extracted on my own and checked out with Gary. We agreed that there was not enough data. Still, Gary and I soon reached an understanding that chemotherapy was appropriate. As to the choice between a radical and functional dissection, we agreed that this was a matter for clinical judgment.

Radical dissection would have no effect on distant metastases. However, the chemotherapy might have an effect. As for local control, the regional and functional dissections again were the same. Chemotherapy could improve the odds of local control. These effects would be mitigated to a finite yet uncertain degree because local and regional radiation had shrunk or destroyed my capillaries and chemotherapy depends on the chemicals delivered via the capillaries.

Although I was complicit in the butchery of my own body, I had no time for tears. I was cold and brutal with myself, and I will ever be grateful to Gary for sharing the coldness of the analysis, if not its brutality. Through discussions with him, I developed a coherent way of thinking about the alternatives and likelihoods of outcomes necessary to both my health and sanity.

A physician can approach cancer alternatives through the eyes of medical assessment. A layman can approach them as a matter of God's will. An insurance company can approach them as costs. A family member can approach them with hope. The approach depends on one's position. I had chosen my way of dealing — research, learning, consultation, assessment, evaluating odds, et cetera — and I lived to conclude that it was the right way not just for me, but a way that others might usefully employ, especially today with the internet.

The week before the surgery, I gave Sasaki my decision: a functional dissection with adjuvant chemotherapy. The surgery itself would be safe; postsurgical events would be dealt with as they happened. Chemotherapy would extend for twenty-one courses weekly with a week's respite after every two weeks. Fisher recommended chemotherapy with Ronald DeConti, a former student of his at the Albany Medical Center.

Although I was being passed around from best of hands to the best of hands, my situation was growing dangerous.

CHAPTER 18

Berkeley: The '60s

And then there is that remarkable landscape of space and time I remember simply as "Berkeley." In July 1964, I arrived at the house next to Tilden Park in the Berkeley hills, the first of many places I would live while attending graduate school. Compared to the parks I had known, Tilden was more like a forest preserve than a park. One day, shortly after my arrival in Berkeley, I ventured into Tilden. The grass was a brown peculiar in this country to a California summer and although I walked some four hours I never pierced the innards of this huge park.

Overlooking the East Bay from heights of rugged elegance, Tilden is the crown jewel that connects to a system of other parks that encircle Berkeley, Oakland, and small towns like connective tissue. The whole arrangement perches on the eastern side of San Francisco Bay, a uniquely American variant of European parks that include the Vienna Woods, which has also inhibited suburban sprawl.

San Francisco Bay connects to a Pacific Ocean that had been an abstraction to me. In the months that followed I was to find that it connected to the bodily fluids of many Californians. The Pacific Ocean is as different from the Atlantic Ocean as tea is from coffee. Yes, of course California is a different country.

Up until then, my life had been shaped and limited by my dystonia and how others viewed it. I was never sure in what ways the shaping and limits were fashioned by others or were my own. At twenty-one, I had no conception of work, career, or much of life beyond school. So naturally I continued going to school. But even in graduate school, I was not a typical graduate student. I was too inexperienced to know that the name of the game was to find a mentor and a narrow topic of study in which to excel and so finally be recommended for a job at a prestigious university. If I had known these things, I would have either given it up or developed into a stunted professor; I would never have grown up.

Ever aware that the surgeries for my dystonia had commuted my death sentence and that every year that I lived was a gift and further some sort of indication of a future life, I resolved not to waste my miracle. I resolved to live. Aware of what other people had given to me, I resolved not to return the favor, but to pass the torch. As I became more aware of the stakes, my decision became more conscious and definite. I would live out my delayed adolescence first and let being a graduate student take second place.

That summer I moved in half a dozen different directions. I became an intellectual citizen of the university and joined Berkeley's civil rights movement. I hung out on Telegraph Avenue, experimented with drugs and became part of the nascent hippie culture. I took hikes and walks and saw a shrink to whom Solnit had referred me and hitchhiked around Berkeley then around California. I made friends, developed relationships with women and became a sexual being. This list grew and grew. Was I trying out different lives? Was my personality hopelessly fragmented? Truly, it was neither ... and both. I was growing up, testing myself and testing and tasting the world in giant bites.

I descended from my perch in the Berkeley hills into the flatlands of Berkeley. First I went to the campus. Compared to Yale, the architecture was dreadful. But the campus was beautiful and reeked with bizarre vegetation. There were nooks for the intellect and crannies for the senses. Although Cal, as Berkeley is known in Berkeley, was not laid out with the forethought of genius of Central Park, it worked, and its jungle accomplished what no ivy had ever done for Yale.

I made many excursions into the lowlands of Berkeley and got to know some of my future professors. These were largely in political science. The ones who impressed me the most were in political theory.

Politics, in its broadest sense, shaped my long-postponed growing up. I was in the right place at the right time with the right set of intellectual interests. My first intellectual efforts were critical of political science and that was my first hook. I gave up on my plan to be a mathematical political scientist.

During the summer of '64 I joined Berkeley campus CORE (Congress of Racial Equality) and made my first progressive friends. There was Jack Weinberg who soon impressed me as a political organizer and Barbara Garson in whose Delaware Street house we had meetings and who was soon to impress others as the author of *MacBird*, an attack on the Johnson administration. Her then-husband, Marvin, was in Texas with Mark Lane investigating conspiracy theories around the Kennedy assassination.

At the end of that summer we all headed south to Watts in Los Angeles to attend a statewide meeting of CORE. A political expert, Jack brought along a ditto machine and typewriter. We were the only delegation at the meeting with the power of the media, however minor. Jack's skills as an organizer and Barbara's skills as a propagandist gave us an influence beyond our importance. At crucial times we controlled the meeting.

During subsequent episodes of white liberal guilt, I've had occasion to question our power. But the upshot of that meeting was that California CORE emerged a far stronger organization at a time when strength was needed. I drew satisfaction from playing a part in doing good with others and for others.

Given my sheltered upbringing, it was the first time that I had been close to and worked with blacks for any length of time. The second evening a woman named Savannah threw a party in her room. The motel was modest; the room was small, and we all squeezed in on Savannah's bed. As Savannah fussed with my curly hair, she exclaimed, "Why, you must be part black." Physical closeness, I learned, was a good way to learn about being close. The meeting was held in Watts, and I took some time off to see the Watts towers, among the few of this country's monumental public art works of genius. There were many lessons here: significance from insignificance, creativity without education, sumptuousness amidst poverty ... and much more. We drove the freeway back to Berkeley, singing proud about ourselves and what we had done. I am lucky to have lived during the years when *Black and White Together* were more than the lyrics of a song.

While still living in a commune in the Berkeley hills in '64, I met Moses. Still in his teens, Moses had a body shaped like mine, a flat-chested mesomorph, but where my body was of modest size his was huge. Where mine was disabled his was able-bodied. He had none of the graduate student trappings that I had, none of the social consciousness. This giant was from the Berkeley of runaways, drugs, and hippiedom.

Moses was definitely uncommitted. Moses also may have been a sociopath. We fascinated each other. Moses became my route to many experiences that would otherwise have remained foreign. Some of these experiences I encountered directly, others vicariously. For example, because Moses attracted women effortlessly, I got vicarious inklings of the world of sex. Further, Moses was something of an outlaw. He had the distinction of being told by the Berkeley police to be out of town before sundown.

Berkeley was still part of the Wild West. To me the West was fiction, properly relegated to films. It caught me unaware that there *was* a West, a frontier, a discovery that the rest of the country made when it elected as president sometimes B western movie star Ronald Reagan.

One evening, I was on the back of a Vespa motor scooter driven by

Moses on the way to a party. A policeman stopped us and asked us what we were about. He told us to turn around and searched us both for weapons. I couldn't believe it. Then he came to a pocket in my jacket. He felt something hard. He stepped back, took out his gun and aimed it at me.

"Take that out slowly." He said gesturing towards my pocket.

How preposterous that I with my ragged movements could do anything slowly. I managed to retrieve the screwdriver that Moses had given me in case the cantankerous motor scooter stalled again. As I took out the screwdriver the policeman said, "That is a deadly weapon."

The feeling of having a gun aimed at me is with me to this day. I don't like it. My grandfather's story had taught me about the power of the state and my father and mother had lived in a state drunk with power. At that moment, I learned the lesson of the absolute power of the state for myself.

As my first school year approached, I moved to my own apartment on Telegraph Avenue, not yet either famous or infamous. Above Moe's Books, the apartment's oak floors were painted black, which surprised me. I was used to oak floors being waxed or varnished or covered with 1950s wall-to-wall carpeting. I did not know that painting floors was what poor people did. No longer were most of the lessons in my life coming through my formal education. It was a change I was aware of, treasured, and cultivated.

Down the hall from me above Moe's lived a woman named Michelle. Although not typically Californian, Michelle could not have been from any other part of the country. Her lightness of spirit, and the litheness that informed her walk were combined with an obliqueness of speech and a hippieness of dress. She had a particularly Californian relationship to the ocean. I, who had spent many weekends at Atlantic beaches, thought that I had known the ocean. But California women at times resonate the Pacific, and if you put your head to their breasts you will hear the sounds of the sea as clearly as if you put your head to a seashell.

The slowness of the pace in California struck me. New Yorkers could take it over. I didn't realize that they had. Further, I didn't realize that California had, in turn, taken over those New Yorkers who had taken her over.

My excellent education at Yale prepared me too well and my first semester went too easily. I found the field of quantitative political science simply did not exist at Cal. Ernest Haas was no Karl Deutsch, despite Karl's recommendation of him. The only way for me to engage in quantitative political science was to engage in the econometric political science of Herb McClosky. Econometrics is a branch of statistics, and statistics is a branch of mathematics that, unlike most subjects mathematical, held little appeal for me.

Although there were no Lindbloms, Deutsches, or Dahls at Berkeley, there was a great and magical cohort of what political scientists call political theorists. At Yale, political theory was the understanding of ideology. At the same time, the political theorist Leo Strauss was culturing a cult that later became the influential and notorious neoconservatives. At Berkeley the goal of political theory was no less than to make the world more decent, politics more democratic. This, in part, involved me in a critique of the current world.

Most political scientists dismissed political theory as "normative," at best as value laden, at worst as ideology or propaganda — a dismissal that presumes that political science is a true science. That some practitioners of political science at Berkeley made this claim with no idea of what science really meant revolted me and insulted the scientific part of my education.

I was forced into political theory partly because of my disgust at these outrageous claims and partly because I was drawn to it by an extraordinary faculty. Norman Jacobson, John Schaar, and Sheldon Wolin, names that today are largely unknown, were legendary at Berkeley and the people who bore them were exemplary. Their breadth of knowledge, wisdom and imagination dominated much intellectual life at Berkeley. Although becoming a disciple or a groupie is far from my nature, these men had a profound effect on my life.

My work went well, except for Constitutional Law, which did not attract me. The teacher, Professor Aiken, encouraged me to hook up with Professor TenBroek. Only much later, after I left Berkeley and TenBroek died of cancer, did I become aware he had founded the National Federation for the Blind and had been active in disability law. An opportunity missed. Another opportunity missed was my classmate, Ed Roberts, who was historically one of the most significant figures in the disability rights movement in which I later became involved. Although Ed and I were not close at the time, many years later I was happy to recommend him for a MacArthur Fellowship that he received.

Winters in Berkeley are not white, they're gray, and the winter's damp rain is bone cold. And so it was that during winter break, I paid fifty dollars for a drive away car whose owner wanted it delivered to New York, and Moses and a friend of his took turns driving the car from California. We left early in the morning and drove across country. As we did not eat, our restroom stops grew further apart.

We got into Manhattan close to two o'clock in the morning and headed for Greenwich Village. We closed the Feenjon coffee house and then casually roamed around Manhattan's streets. We headed to Third Avenue and Tenth Street to spend the night at the east coast branch of a commune called Kerista. Years later when I lived in an apartment around the corner on East Eleventh Street, I went to see if Kerista still existed. Nobody had heard of it.

My friend from Yale, Gary Saxonhouse, invited me to a New Year's party at his cousin's apartment. I took Moses and his friend along and within an hour these burly, dashing hippies from the west coast had each snatched a woman. And so did I. Her name was Irene, and we left the party for her apartment. Although neither of us were virgins, we were both surely amateurs. We started off clumsily, but as we progressed we became proficient lovers.

When we first began, I was drugging and drinking. After I got used to Irene and she to me, I needed neither drugs nor alcohol. My dystonic tremors folded into the rhythms of love making, harkening back to the roots of my neurology. I not only learned about Irene and making love, but about my body. This time I entered my body through the portal of eroticism. None of this was a surprise. It was a gracious remembering of my erotic body. We did not leave the bed for three days and three nights except to pee. I was surprised to discover that sexual activity closed off hunger for both of us. In finding Irene, I was supremely lucky. I remain grateful to Irene for what she taught me about herself and about me. Sex remains important to me not just for the usual reasons, but also as a way for my body to explore itself. Sex was one of the few physical activities at which I was genuinely good and a fine reminder that I was not a disembodied brain. I left New York an experienced political body, social body, sexual body, and for the first time, a thoroughly lived body.

Back in Berkeley I took my thoroughly lived body through a one-credit course in wrestling. I was frequently matched against a proficient wrestler, far larger and stronger than I and to whom I invariably lost. No matter. I was not wrestling to win. I was wrestling to be close to another body, to smell our mingled sweat, to push and pull as hard as I could. I learned more about my own body, and, as well, about a wisdom my body lacked. Although in theory, I was entirely familiar with the physics of wrestling and knew what had to be done in each situation, I was consistently clobbered.

My time at Berkeley included the sex and drugs for which, among other things, the 1960s is blamed and credited. The '60s could not have been the '60s without drugs. But drugs had a social context and meant different things in the '60s than they mean now. For example, big time crime had not gotten into the distribution of marijuana. Consuming marijuana did not contribute to corruption. In Berkeley marijuana was common. Speed and heroin were proscribed; cocaine was uncommon; crack non-existent. In my travels back and forth from East Coast to West Coast, I learned that drugs had a social context and that when it came to drugs, the East and the West were two different nations.

That first autumn at Berkeley, I had my first and only encounter with LSD. With the idea that being close to nature was a good thing with drugs, a group of us took it in Tilden Park. As the LSD took effect, I seemed to be shrinking. The grass seemed to grow from my ankles to over my shoulders. I was a four year old. We descended from Berkeley hills into a house in the flats. I went into the bathroom and turned on the light. The figure in the mirror was a changed one. He was suffering yet beautiful and, unavoidably, me.

Later I lay on a mattress in the living room listening to the Beatles and a Bartok Quartet. I was inside the sound being emitted from each instrument. I learned how to listen to music. I took a book with some paintings by Michelangelo off the table and looked at them. They looked different to me than they normally would have. They were deeper. The spaces became as important as what filled them. I learned to listen to music and to look at art. Then I started writhing on the floor. In my pocket, I had a Thorazine pilfered from my father's office just in case of a bad trip. I swallowed it and within half an hour was asleep. I did not take LSD again.

Although I did frequently smoke marijuana, I never came close to being a pothead. I learned about the sexual properties of marijuana, the heightened senses, what it could do to music, et cetera. For me, sex and drugs were just parts of life as it existed in the '60s. My time included much else and growing up involved far more.

In the autumn of 1964 the university attempted to close down the political tables that historically had set up in the plaza off the main entrance to the University that leads to Telegraph Avenue. I was a member of CORE, and the CORE table was a target of the administration. A police car materialized in Sproul Hall Plaza and the police plunked a bemused Jack Weinberg into the back seat. But the vehicle was not about to depart as a group of students, myself among them, encircled the car. The circle drew more students to it and soon the police car was an island in a Pacific Ocean of students. One by one, the students mounted the car and gave speeches. Although Sproul Plaza, as it was known, was never designed for rallies and demonstrations, it is perfectly constructed for these events. The plaza has easy access to a major street on one side, steps on the second, a gateway to the rest of the campus on the third, and impressive steps to the Administration Building on the fourth. It was to become the major public space at the university.

Soon there were thousands of students. Students mounted the police car with Weinberg inside to give speeches. After a while, some faculty members gingerly did the same. Later, a series of speakers mounted Sproul Hall steps. One of them, Mario Savio, likened the University to a machine. Although that did not feel true for me, it resonated with the feelings of others. And if the University were a machine, it would never again be allowed to run without question.

I was one of the first students to surge into Sproul Hall. It was the first time I had ever seen so many people together, each one acting for the benefit of the others. It was a community. Well before Joan Baez from nearby Carmel joined to sing there were many performances of various sorts. In another room there were political speeches. It was as if the whole world was in the building.

The sit-in at Sproul Hall was a powerful experience for everyone involved. For me, perhaps the most profound effect was to render arguments against Utopian possibilities false. After all, here was one. From now on I had to take the idea of Utopia seriously. It was time to reflect on, if not jettison, my feelings about the natural barbarism of human beings, a legacy of my father's experiences with anti–Semitism in Austria.

I had been awake a long time and that night I left for home planning to come back after a good night's sleep. There was nothing to come back to. Late that night the police came and arrested the students whom I was later told became the most studied group of students in history.

The Free Speech Movement, F.S.M. for short, was born and Cal broke open the '60s. Many Cal students were radicalized. Faculty resolutions were made and a new college was launched in its spirit. Students became expert at organizing press conferences and themselves. Although we had factions, they were incorporated into an organic leadership chosen from among us. A steering committee emerged whose spokesman was Mario Savio, a man of much principle who would later withdraw from Berkeley politics for a time when he became the subject of a cult of personality.

Although I was a vitally engaged and committed participant in the free speech movement leadership, I was an outsider. Perhaps this was because I simply did not know how to be part of a group. Certainly my disability had prevented me from learning many of even the most basic social lessons. Or perhaps it was because I could not submerge my individuality to a group. I never was sure when I had said something brilliant and or when others pretended I had because I had a disability. Or perhaps I was a Groucho Marxist, who would not be a member of any group that accepted me. Too many possibilities float around the soup. Whatever my personal standing, the big picture was clear. Conventional social structure lay in shreds, and a tapestry of democratic community had replaced it. There was no going back.

CHAPTER 19

Warrior, August 1988

My body was a house of violence at the cellular level. Speaking of my cancer as a battle and using the vocabulary of war did not come easily to me. But to be in a violent situation with closed eyes is dangerous. The facts demanded the war imagery that became a natural, constructive way for me to think about it.

Early on the morning of the functional neck dissection, Lew appeared at my bedside and said, "I think we're doing the right thing."

"I think so too."

"My patients are just next door," Lew said. "I'll be dropping in a lot."

"I know. Thanks."

An attendant wheeled me downstairs into a large room where other patients also awaited surgery. Before I was rolled into the operating theater, an attendant verified my name. Following his cue, and not from paranoia, but from the knowledge that hospitals sometimes make mistakes, I asked, "Do you have me down for a functional dissection?" He glanced at my chart and confirmed, "Dr. Sasaki. Functional neck dissection."

After some fifteen minutes I was wheeled into a large operating room. Sasaki and the resident were talking at the far side of the room. Even in surgical scrubs, Sasaki was handsome. He came over, smiled and said, "You will just feel a prick in the hand."

The neck bone connected to the head bone ... and all the nerves from the body in between run through the narrow neck. Not a lot of working room, but ample room for fatal slips. Over the next five hours, Sasaki carefully exposed layer after layer and worked his way down until the lymphatic chain was exposed and carefully removed.

I woke up in the recovery room with fullness in my bladder and a balloon catheter. Still groggy from the anesthesia, although I was not joyous that I was alive, I did, however, take note of my life. Back in my room, my mother was waiting for me. "Sasaki called to let me know everything went well," she said. "He said the node was grossly encapsulated."

This was good news. An encapsulated node meant that on clinical inspection the cancer was trapped in this one node. A malignant node forms a capsule around it to shield the cancer cells from the normal defenses of the body. When the cancer cells are ready, the capsule breaks, and they continue their spread through the body.

My neck ached, but that was to be expected. Demerol was on my schedule and I did not and would not use it for pain. I would use it to get high because there are few things I dislike as much as being in hospitals. I slipped in and out of sleep until a nurse woke me the next morning to take my vital signs.

Unlike my last hospital visit for the radium implants, this time I was not radioactive. Now my hospital room was a veritable revolving door that delivered a steady stream of visitors and staff. When Lew came in, he said, "Everything went fine. I was in yesterday to see you, but you were asleep. How are you feeling?"

"All right," I answered. Of course, what I meant was: as well as could be expected. I did not feel like getting up and dancing.

Lew said, "You'll be feeling a lot better in a few days."

"I know."

"Anything I can do for you?" he asked.

"No, thanks. I made it, huh?" I ventured.

"You made it," said Lew.

Next came the intern who read my chart and looked at my wound. Plastic drainage tubes sat under the tissue. From my reading, I knew that over the next few days new connecting tissue would generate between the flap and the underlying flesh. He checked my I.V.s.

"What's in there?" I asked.

"Your breakfast."

"Anything else?"

"Keflex ... antibiotics to be sure an infection doesn't develop."

Next an Ear, Nose, and Throat resident appeared. He repeated the intern's examination, read the intern's notes and entered his own notes. He took a closer more practiced look at the wound, pronounced, "Doing fine," and then left.

Within half an hour, a ring of ENT residents on rounds squeezed into the room. Sasaki was at the back. The resident who had been to see me earlier reported to the group about my progress. He turned to me and asked, "Do you have any questions?"

"No."

As the group left the room, Sasaki was the last one out. I had saved one question for him. "Did you get everything you wanted to?" I asked.

"Yes," Sasaki answered, then he smiled. "You have a big mastoid muscle." I had heard that during surgery Sasaki had trouble pushing my "markedly developed mastoid," as Cooper had termed it, out of the way.

Surgery had cancelled my long anticipated trip to see Daniel at the Farm and Wilderness Camp in Vermont. Although the loss was a real blow for me, I was more worried about Daniel. Hoping for the best, I had written him a letter outlining what happened and had given it to Judith to deliver to him on visiting day. When Judith came to visit me at the hospital — after oddly spending the night in a hotel rather than at my mother's house — I asked, "How did things go with Daniel?"

"All right," she said. "I told him that you had been operated on. I was with him when he read your letter. Everything seemed to go fine."

Relief coursed through me.

During my stay in the hospital, I formed a deep bond with many of my nurses who ran the gamut from the Wicked Witch of the West to Dorothy. This bonding would not have been possible without the continual presence of my mother, sister and the rest of my family whose active presence brought out the best in the nurses.

My stay was uneventful with the exception that my prostate was injured by the insertion of the Foley balloon catheter. After they took it out, I could not urinate. I filed that bit of information away for future reference.

Finally the time came to remove the tubes that secured the flap to the rest of me. Staples in my neck, I was discharged in a combination of post surgical technique, economics, medicine, and a bureaucracy of accounting which paid by the procedure. As usual, five days in bed was enough to make me forget how to walk.

My cousin, Ernie, drove me home to Albany where Judith had been furiously preparing for the opening of her new art show that night. She was one of the best artists in Albany and Ernie and I stopped off at the gallery before the show and admired her work. She had gone to the country to rest up for her show and Ernie helped me into our painfully empty house. That evening, weak, tired and very alert, I dragged my exhausted mangled body to the show. The opening went well. Judith glowed; I flickered.

Ten days later I took the bus back to New Haven to have the staples removed from my neck. Sasaki examined me and was satisfied. "Pathology found the cancer limited to one node," he said. "But I sent it back for double-checking and they found a small hole in the capsule."

I clicked the safety off. The cancer might have escaped from its capsule. This reaffirmed my decision to go ahead with the chemotherapy.

After my visit with Sasaki, I stopped in at Lew's office. Lew had me move my head in various ways and performed a brief neurological exam. He was satisfied that not much damage had been done.

Next I gave Dave Fisher a call, and he squeezed me in. I only needed a couple of minutes. "What do you think my chances of a five year survival are?" I asked.

"I can't say," said Fisher.

"I'm not asking for a judgment based on the fact," I said, "I'm just asking for a guess based on your wisdom." I was pushing, and he knew it. He allowed me to push.

"I would say about seventy percent," he said. "That's not science, you understand. That's a guess."

"I know." I said. "I respect your guesses, and that's all I was asking for. Seven out of ten seems like pretty good odds to me." If the cancer was spreading, it would spread fast, and I wanted to make sure I had cleaned up all the details. "If things don't work out, I may not have the chance to say this to you. I want to thank you for all you've done, and I appreciate the time you spent with me."

Like a soldier breaking down his weapon and checking his gear, I ran over my checklist. I did not know what the next year would hold for me and I was worried about Daniel. Back in Albany, I called Marlissa Parker, Daniel's old principal, and asked a favor. Could she get Daniel into Mrs. Hyslop's fourth grade section? These were extraordinary times and Daniel should have the most mature, accomplished teacher possible. Marlissa understood extraordinary times — two years before she had lost a husband to cancer. She said not to worry; it would be done.

Next I dropped down into the big ugly to see Ronald DeConti. In the weeks and months to come, the ugliness of the chemotherapy suite deep in the bowels of the Albany Medical Center would become more and more offensive to me. In contrast to his wretched surroundings, Dr. DeConti was an attractive man about ten years my senior who resembled Marcello Mastroianni. He was a warm, caring physician and a good doctor. Once again, I was in the best of hands. "There is a fifty percent chance that you have no cancer," he said. "In that case, chemotherapy would be unnecessary. If you do have some cancer, there's about a fifty percent chance of the chemotherapy getting it. There is no way to be certain that chemotherapy is your best chance except if it fails and the cancer returns." I would never know if the chemotherapy worked, only if it didn't. Although we were playing with only a twenty-five percent chance of necessary efficacy, that made it worthwhile.

DeConti performed the thorough physical of a good medical, not surgical, person. I had to be in good shape for the chemotherapy. Not only was DeConti a fit medical man, he proved a tolerable psychiatrist who had an oncologist's familiarity with death. I found myself talking to him about things that mattered to me, like living to see Daniel go to college, not being particularly afraid of death, lying versus the truth should events take a turn for the worse, et cetera.

Although DeConti might easily have avoided such discussions, he didn't. Cancer brings its own camaraderie, and I discovered how easy it was to talk about anything to people who knew cancer or who had been involved in war or other dramatic life-threatening situations. Regrettably, this meant that there were people I could not talk to.

Over the next few days of getting back to work and home, I was much more tired than I expected. But I had the immense satisfaction of knowing that my decisions were well researched, thoughtful and on target. I thought I had done pretty much everything right. I had the hyper-vigilance of a soldier on watch and a new directness — or was it boldness? I had changed deeply, irreversibly, and for the better. I had become courageous, and I acted and continued to act with courage. I say this not grandly, but honestly and simply. I had become a warrior.

CHAPTER 20

American in Paris, 1966–1967

In 1965 I applied to Cal for an advanced traveling fellowship to study in Paris the next year. This was in the days before I had mastered many of the practical details of living. I did not yet know how to do laundry, plan ahead, or come up with alternative plans. In those post–Cooper brain surgery days, I was still getting used to the idea of having a future and still more certain of getting an award than of growing another year older.

Although I did not make alternate plans, still, I was surprised when I received the official letter of award, which was signed by Clark Kerr. Sanford Elberg, the Dean of Graduate Studies, invited me to his office and enjoyed himself immensely during our talk. He clearly relished being able to open a new door to me and apparently had a large part in engineering the award. He wanted me to get every benefit from being in Paris. The Cite Universitaire on the fringes of Paris consisted of many buildings, each belonging to a country that had sent students to Paris to study. I stayed at the American House there.

At that time, the French government provided luxuriously for the students, and I took many of my meals at student cafeterias. I developed my first appreciation for good food and discovered that almost everything was more delicious if undercooked by American standards. I fell into the French habit of drinking a carafe of red wine with each meal and developed a particular fondness for French stews of kidney and of beef. My childhood openness to new and different foods allowed me an easy and appreciative expansion into the French diet. I ate well and lived well and learned much from my professors, friends, and from Paris itself.

I metabolized Paris at the cellular level and reveled in walking her streets. Often I set off with no other objective than to be out walking in that beautiful world. Gradually, these walks became longer and longer as I soaked in the architecture, the light and the style of the city and its people. The grand buildings of Paris had not yet been cleaned and still bore a gray, centuries-old patina.

French women took great care with their sexuality and even those of modest means would own at least one smashing outfit, which they would mend and clean as required. As sophisticated as the French women were in their sexuality, I was unsophisticated. I also did not know the social rituals that devolved on sex. I slunk away in rejection when one girl declined a dinner invitation and added, "But I would be happy to have dinner with you next week." I dated another woman for weeks unaware that I was expected to make erotic advances. So after a while, she stopped seeing me.

My spoken French was soon without American accent. My professors were superb. I took a course in anthropology with Claude Levi-Strauss, a course in international relations with Raymond Aaron, and a course in modern art with Jean Cassou. At school, I characteristically had few obligations and many intellectual opportunities.

I lived a rich intellectual and politically alive international life. In addition to the friends I made at the Cite Universitaire, I made numerous friends in Paris proper. There was the artist Michel Cuchat, Mimi Rewald, the cousin of Arlene Saxonhouse, the social psychologist Serge Moscovici, the karate master and student of English, Ernest Sturm, and many others.

My French friends accused me of living in an uncivilized country and taunted me with the Watts riots and Viet Nam. At a party I met Nancy Nolting, a beautiful young dancer whose father had been ambassador to Viet Nam until Kennedy kicked him out. I remember Nancy saying, "It was so possible when it was Diem." At that same party, I also met Davida Fineman, a communist who had graduated from Cornell during the period that drove the conservative Allan Bloom berserk. Two years later she would show up in Berkeley, and we would become friends. But for the moment we were content to leave Michel's together at four in the morning and go from cafe to cafe. In one, a French artist mocked my disability. He recited what his hands could do that mine could not and then compounded his insult by making a play for Davida. Although my hands could not do many of the things he mentioned, they could — and should — have belted him. I knew I could deck him, but I have never belted anyone.

As the French winter hit, the temperature in my room dropped. It was so cold, I was forced to masturbate vigorously each morning to stop my shivering as it was the first exercise that I could do without getting out from under the covers. In October, I was struck with a sudden fever that removed my rationality too quickly to take the antibiotics that my father had given me.

To this day, I do not travel without them. I checked into a French hospital, which served the Cite Universitaire. They placed me in a room with a man from New Caledonia who had a swollen tongue and who died eight hours later. The next day they changed the sheets and replaced the dead man with a Canadian. In the meantime, I saw nothing sterilized.

For two days I waited for medical intervention that never came. On the third morning, my fever broke and I could again think clearly. Seeing that nothing was being done for me and reckoning that my life would be best served by getting out of the hospital, I snuck out in my pajamas at five in the morning and made my escape. Still shivering with fever in the pre-dawn light, I made my way back to my tiny room at the Cite Universitaire and put myself on the antibiotics that my father had provided me. Within two days, I felt better.

French hospitals should not have surprised me. Earlier, in the fall, I had made the acquaintance of French bureaucracy. Up until that time, perhaps my disability had insulated me from learning certain basics of living like how to fill out forms and fit into bureaucracies. Always a fan of advanced courses, I now took a self-taught graduate crash course in international bureaucracy.

Bureaucracies are artifacts created by people with certain purposes in mind, not the least of which is domination. Bureaucracy, like baseball, is an artificial game from which certain groups — such as those with disabilities — may be excluded. To the degree that bureaucracies are interested in people, they're interested only in some abstracted version of an average bureaucratic person — a case. This means that people with disabilities are likely to find themselves canaries in a coalmine at the mercy of bureaucracies that are at varying times and in varying degrees difficult, appalling or impossible.

All this being said, French bureaucracy makes American bureaucracy blush for its lack of red tape to cover it. To stay in France for more than three months I needed a residence visa. To obtain this visa I reported to the appropriate building. Because of the confusing location of the offices, it was only with some difficulty that I reached the correct floor. The corridor went on and on and turned the corner. None of the doors were marked.

Which of the many doors should I go through? I didn't have a clue. I went through the nearest door where there was a pile of people in a huge room busily going through a pile of papers.

"Excuse me," I said in my perfect spoken French, "Can you tell me, which room for a residence visa?"

In the United States they would have either known or known where to go to ask. The woman behind the desk invited me to go back downstairs and start all over again. Talking with cases was simply not her job.

As I had no intention of doing that, I crossed the narrow corridor into another room and asked again.

"Room 798 is around the corner and across the hall," the man behind the desk assured me. "They can help you there."

As I limped back and forth across the hall from room to room, I began to feel as if I were trapped in a cartoon. Although Inspector Clouseau had not yet reached the screen, his clumsiness, which I possess in spades, quickly constellated within the French bureaucratic environment to result in a similar ludicrous reality. Disabled people are simply too diverse to fit easily into bureaucracies.

I went to Room 798 and said to the man behind the desk, "I've come for a residence visa. Can you help me?"

I stood waiting for an answer.

The man behind the desk returned to work. I didn't know what to do. A man at another desk in the same room asked, "Can I help you?" Perhaps he was exceeding his job description.

A friend! I stated my business.

"You want Room 732."

I went to 732.

The man behind the desk said, "Ah, this is the correct room, but it's the wrong time. Business such as yours is only attended to in the mornings."

I shall refrain from the rest of the story.

The upshot was that I discovered if I left the country before my visa expired, I could avoid the whole bureaucracy. So every three months, I left the country.

My first bureaucratic breakout was to London, which to my surprise, and the Beatles notwithstanding, I did not enjoy. I found the layout of the city without reason or rhyme and had difficulty walking the cobblestone streets. I hooked up with an American engineering student on her last fling in Europe. I tagged along as she did London, from museum to museum, from sight to sight and had dinner in a pretentious Italian restaurant where we were overcharged. I stood up, raised my voice, thought my disapproval in French, and translated it into English. I was shocked when the waiter excused us from the bill without any fight. He was too well behaved, docile, even. No self-respecting French waiter would ever do that without at least some expression of resistance.

With more than my fill of indecent English cuisine under my belt, I headed back to my cheap hotel to pack for Paris.

Three months later at the next "visa break," I found myself on my way to Germany with Sylvia, an emotionally ragged lesbian suffering through the tail end of a love affair. Sylvia and I both spoke fluent German. Her parents had immigrated to the United States from Austria at about the same time as my parents.

On the train to Berlin we shared a compartment with a German woman. As we went through the Alsace region some workmen got on. Bourgeois that we were, we thwarted their efforts to pick up the woman. As we were sitting on the bench across from hers, we forestalled their attempts simply by engaging the woman in conversation. A young German man got on the train in time to witness our rescue. Fifty miles later, after the workmen got off, the woman asked, "Where are you from?"

Sylvia answered easily, "The United States."

"How can you speak such good German then?"

"My parents came from Germany before the war, and we spoke German at home." I knew that Sylvia's answer revealed that we were Jewish.

At the West German border, a guard entered our compartment and asked for passports. The German woman pointed at me and snarled, "He wanted to throw me out the window, and the woman wanted to steal my money!"

When I asked the German man to explain to the passport officer what had really happened, to my astonishment, the man said in German, "I'm not getting mixed up in this." With a shock, I recognized the stereotype of a good German who followed directives.

For the second time in my life, I found myself facing down the barrel of a gun.

At the moment, I did not think about all my parents had gone through to escape Germany and get me into this life, or all the surgeries I had gone through to save that life, or about the French bureaucracy that had driven me into this compartment on this train to Berlin to face anti–Semitism and a German gun. In typical fashion, I split into two people, one of whom was entirely detached and rational — and another who was a passive, emotional object.

It ended well. The passport officer separated us from the Germans. The two Germans were escorted to their own compartment, and Sylvia and I were left alone. We stretched ourselves out on the benches and tried to sleep. The passport officer at the East German border was a middle-aged woman, no doubt a Communist Party member. In contrast to the West German guard, her gruff but proper manner was a welcome relief.

This was one of my first clear experiences of anti–Semitism. The incident made me wonder. Had my disability protected me from other experiences of anti–Semitism? And, if so, how many and how much?

Because of my disability I cannot drive and had gotten used to hitchhiking as a substitute. But Berlin was an island in its own Red Sea, and I soon realized that there was no way out. My claustrophobia intensified when two brand new Leica cameras and several lenses appeared on the bureau of our hotel room. Sylvia was a kleptomaniac. I needed out.

Poland! I would go to Poland.

I presented myself to the Polish consulate, an uneven, distressed, disabled student who often jerked when anxious, wanting to go to Poland without having declared that intention on his way out of the United States. The bureaucrat at the desk said that I would have to talk to the cultural attaché. The attaché, obviously a spy, reminded me of my Polish grandfather in his more secretive moments. The resemblance prompted me to occasional outbursts of cackling that did not add to my value as a prospective guest. The attaché and I had a long discussion about why I wanted to go to Poland. My answers did not convince him. Finally, desperate, I said, "Adam Schaaf invited me."

He perked up. Adam Schaaf was a member of the Communist Party Central Committee. "And how do you know him?"

"He spoke to my class at Yale University." I spoke the truth.

The attaché was left with the bureaucratic choice of having to check out my story or let me go. He gave me the visa.

Still, I arrived at Checkpoint Charlie after twelve o'clock on Saturday and would have had to stay in Berlin until Monday. Visions of Sylvia's kleptomania embroiling me in the vast police department danced in my head. Instead of waiting, I got on the first plane out of Berlin, which was to Copenhagen, and after two days of insipid Danish modern, flew back to Paris.

My third escape from bureaucracy was a riotous tour with fourteen French students to Greece and Israel. Our first stop was Athens. Awkwardly, I scrambled up the uneven, decaying steps to the Acropolis. I was not sure-footed, my dystonia had caused me many pratfalls from grace, and I suffered from an entirely justified fear of heights. Despite having taken an undergraduate course in Greek art, I was unprepared for the overwhelming effect it had on me. The Greek light, architecture and art all dazzled. While I stood on the heights of the Acropolis with Athens at my feet, the cradle rocked. The broken sound of far off shouts seeped through the air. Occasionally, there was a firecracker or a gunshot. A revolution was going on. The crowds were calling for a long-time economist from Berkeley, Andraeus Papendreau, as Prime Minister.

The French students I was traveling with, even those who had revolutionary sentiments, were increasingly nervous and self-conscious. Like a scene from Genet's *Balcony*, they went on about their sightseeing while Athens was in revolution. Their behavior repelled me, and I left them to descend into the city to see what was going on. In the center of Athens is the Place of

Harmony. Off to one side was a street with thousands chanting, "Papendreau! Papendreau!" I followed the sound and found myself in a crowd reminiscent of Berkeley. I marched with Greek students whom I felt to be compatriots. Shots and tear gas grenades went off in front of the crowd. The crowd started running back down the street. Although normally unable to run, I found myself dancing my way through the crowd, around barriers, and even dodging clubs at the beginning of the street near the Place of Harmony.

What kind of disability was this, never being sure? Had the reversion been to instinct, I could have understood it — maybe. Yet I did not run out of mere instinct. I ran in the way that as a child I had seen the fullbacks run during football games in the Yale Bowl. Had I fallen, I would have been trampled. Had I not dodged, I would have been struck with a club. At the end of the block were men armed with batons and guns.

Off the Place of Harmony was a café. I went in, sat down and ordered ouzo and waited for my heart to stop pounding. Although fully prepared to march with my fellow Greek students, I did not know enough about the situation to know if I wished to make it my fight. Tanks rolled down into the Place of Harmony. Someone lobbed a tear gas grenade into the café. In the years to come I would smell tear gas frequently, although never in such an exquisitely concentrated form. The smell was both unforgettable and disgusting.

Ordinarily, my disability should have made me a helpless victim of the tear gas. But now, I seemed to be acting out a movie and did things that ordinarily I could not do. I recalled the directions for escaping from smoke-filled environments and immediately transferred it to tear gas. With no time for thought and warning myself *not the ouzo not the ouzo,* I tipped over a glass of water on my napkin and held the wet napkin to my eyes. I fell to the floor and crawled out of the cafe. The tear gas was intense. My skin burned.

I trotted back to the hotel to shower off the stinging gas. Greeks with pails of water had stationed themselves on the street corners. Seeing me in agony, they doused me. I said my "thank yous" and went on to my hotel where I gratefully took a shower and went to bed. The next day I read in the English newspapers that the tear gas had killed a Swiss journalist by suffocation.

A few days later, we embarked from Athens' port of Piraeus for Israel. My cabin was next to the hot, noisy engine room so I slept on deck in the perfectly clear air. I had never really believed in the Milky Way nor known how drenched with stars the sky is. I soaked them in. As we traveled from Tel Aviv to Jerusalem to Eilat, I stood in the Dead Sea, went to the oasis at En Geddi, to a kibbutz called Nyat Mordecai, and saw many a sight. But more important than what I saw was what I felt. In that place, I yearned for my ancestors and heard their ghosts around me. This complex frontier country permeated by so many different cultures would always be a home to me if I needed it.

And so, in this way, I avoided French bureaucracy.

CHAPTER 21

Chemical Warfare,
Autumn 1988–Spring 1990

The oppressive heat and humidity of the summer lingered on. Daniel headed into fifth grade as I headed into my first chemo session. By now, I was relying on anyone I could for rides to various medical appointments. Fortunately, the American Cancer Society provided me with rides to cancer-related appointments, and I relied on them to get me to and from chemotherapy.

The chemotherapy suite buried in the basement of the Albany Medical Center was like nothing so much as a dungeon to undergo a modern form of torture. Every week from the autumn of 1988 through the spring of 1990, I returned to the same bleak and revolting waiting room with the same out-of-date insipid magazines and waited to be called out for a blood count to measure my reaction to chemotherapy. Occasionally, the tests involved more extensive blood profiles. Then it was back to the waiting room to what else? ... wait to be called for chemotherapy. The weekly treatment lasted a couple of hours. The television in my cell was invariably tuned to the nurses' favorite, Oprah.

Trying to get a needle into one of my veins is like trying to get a needle into a greased cable in motion. When I sat down at my first chemo session to be connected to the intravenous apparatus and an oncology nurse tried to pierce a vein, it submerged and rolled out of the way. Before coming in for the next session, I took a heavy dose of Compazine with the idea it would relax me enough to make my veins more compliant and would also prevent the nausea that, once triggered, can become a habit for patients in chemo treatment. Yet despite the tranquilizer, my veins still rolled over and hid. It took the nurse six attempts to finally catch them. At the beginning of the fourth session, DeConti sat me down and said, "I've been getting complaints from the nurses about you."

"Me? What did I do?"

"The nurses don't like hurting you. They say you close your eyes and jerk your arms away from them when they try to get a needle into you." I assured him that these movements were involuntary products of my neurology, not pain. Still DeConti insisted the nurses were having trouble. "Why not try a Port-a-Cath(r)?" he said. "It's a little device we can plant under the skin of the chest — then we can just plug you in for chemotherapy." Foolishly, I said, "No."

"The nurses are here to serve *you*," DeConti assured me, "and not vice versa."

I realized that I had not been talking to the nurses enough. I recalled that one of them seemed to find it easier to find my vein, and I suggested to DeConti that we go with her. The circle of patient-nurse-patient now turned from vicious to benign.

Each week after chemo, Dr. DeConti examined me to monitor possible side effects of the chemotherapeutic agents. These exams often involved discussions that ranged from a living will — no dramatic measures, thank you — to what death might mean to me, to the various possibilities of cancer treatment. DeConti handled these sessions with patience and wisdom.

When I got back home, I hit the mattress on my office floor where I now slept and passed out. My experience in the crash pads of the '60s was not wasted.

Over the next weeks and months, an exquisite autumn ripened as I weakened and worsened, and the ugliness of the chemo suite degenerated from merely appalling into gruesome. The treatments matched the surroundings. Contrary to my expectations, these treatments did not become routine with repetition but rather more agonizing. I came to dread the thought of needles going into my veins. I could never be a junkie even if someone with steadier hands than mine did the jabbing.

The chemo treatment process was a methotrexate drip with leucovorin recovery, or to my mind, urine followed by embalming fluid. A high dose of methotrexate, infused over a half-hour period, was the bright golden color of concentrated urine. After this, according to the protocol, I had plain saline for an hour. Then came the 5 FU as a huge syringe of grey embalming fluid was pushed through the IV into my body. The 5 FU was cold and I could feel its coldness radiating into my arms. I felt cold through the whole treatment. I left each session with a lethal dose of methotrexate circulating through my body. I was to walk around with it, a walking time bomb, for twenty-four hours before taking the antidote — a leucovorin tablet, which allowed for higher doses of methotrexate. I found myself in the unnerving position of permitting myself to be poisoned to the point of death and then having to trust a tablet to rescue me. A tablet was such a little thing to hang your life on.

Like a gambler hedging my bets to the side of new age visualizations, I pictured various images during my chemotherapy. But then I hit on a story that was simultaneously powerful and reassuring — the story of Daniel leading his gang of neighborhood friends on flying ET bicycles on a search-and-destroy mission to blast malignant cells. Straight out of *Apocalypse Now*, with Wagner's *Ride of the Valkyrie* playing in the background, they descended howling, destroying first one cell, then another. Sometimes the gang would use chemotherapeutic agents. The urine colored methotrexate was particularly powerful and vulgar. "I piss on you," said Daniel and destroyed a malignant cell. I could count on Daniel, the savage warrior. How I needed him. How he came through.

DeConti insisted I maintain my weight and didn't care what I had to eat to do it. Weight loss could compromise the immune system and also signal a possible recurrence of cancer. Now in complete opposition to everything I knew about nutrition, I was on a high protein, high fat diet — milk shakes, doughnuts, whipped cream, anything and everything. My taste for food changed dramatically. Rare meat was now disgusting. I would not know what I liked, or could even tolerate, until after I had started eating it. I took to eating frozen ravioli with Dijon mustard at each and every dinner, and my diet soon unnerved the organically minded Judith.

I grew increasingly exhausted. DeConti insisted that the tiredness was due to depression. I felt the depression was due to tiredness. The nurses agreed that tiredness was a side effect of chemotherapy. Who to believe? I ended up not caring. Shortly after starting chemotherapy, I went in to see Parnes who made his usual exam. Afterwards, I took out the "thank you" that I had filed away earlier and delivered it. "Thank you," I said.

"For what?"

"You may have saved my life."

Parnes smiled. I left it at that. It was not important for me to know exactly how, to what extent, and in what ways Parnes had had an effect on Sasaki's decision to do a needle biopsy, after initially finding nothing. Something clearly had changed in the equation, and I suspected that Parnes had something to do with it.

Death helped me cut to the chase and allowed me to say what I needed to say.

Most of what I have to say is simple, "I love you," "Thank you," "You're really very helpful," et cetera. I thank people where thanks are due, flatter them where flattery is due, and encourage them where encouragement is due.

I disagree when disagreement is warranted and keep my mouth shut to avoid useless fights. I don't lie.

Now my all-star team included Clarence Sasaki, Yung Son, Steven Parnes, Ronald DeConti, Lewis Levy, Albert Solnit, and Gary Saxonhouse. I played my usual position at right field — a position now important in the major leagues; Oscar Roth played center field; Daniel Roth played left field. This team's success was not measured by the complex statistics so integral to baseball, but by the answer to one simple question: Had it won? The stakes were so high. Was *this* what made the game so exhilarating? Or perhaps, frightening?

I was so exhilarated that I had trouble sleeping. I would wake up during the night on full alert and had trouble falling back to sleep. When I did dream, it was about death and cancer. But though death was a constant companion, suicide was only an abstract option. Although I had built up a stash of Nembutal and Demerol, I did not know if I would be able to swallow them. In retrospect, they served to restore a measure of control in my life. To me, the possibility of suicide was purely hypothetical. Now and in any future that I was prepared to contemplate, my object, my every act, was life.

Unlike Hamlet I had never felt a connection between sleep and death. I, in fact, had preferred many dreams to my waking life, particularly during adolescence when my disability made waking life painful, sleep difficult to achieve, and dreams dramatic and vivid. Now, like Hamlet, I was afraid of sleep because of the dreams that awaited me, afraid too that sleep and death had affinities I had never before truly grasped. Now I understood Hamlet. Like Macbeth, cancer had murdered sleep. But like Yogi Berra, I kept reminding myself, "It ain't over till it's over."

CHAPTER 22

First Person, Political, 1967–1970

In June of 1967, newly returned from Paris, I spent two weeks in New Haven visiting with my parents and friends from Yale, which now seemed somehow changed and outgrown. When I walked in to see Vince Scully, then apostle of modern architecture soon to become apostle of post-modernist architecture, he slid off his chair laughing. To my questioning look, he said, "It's your outfit. It's wonderful, just wonderful."

At that moment, I could see how much I had changed. From the toes up it was a custom made pair of English boots, the first shoes that ever really fit my deformed feet. They zipped up around tight black jeans. The zippers were heavy so that I would not break them when I yanked them up and had leather thongs attached to the pulls so that I could grasp them without falling over. The jeans had a heavy belt with a long buckle that I could close easily and was so large that it covered the button that I could not button. The shirt was a charcoal grey turtleneck, no buttons to worry about.

Really, it *was* wonderful, just wonderful.

My parents welcomed me home with a scolding for worrying them with the tormented tapes I had sent them from Paris. The tapes were replete with meditations on life, death and other unmentionables. They informed me that I should not discuss such subjects with them. Message received, end of tapes, end of trying to convey my feelings to my parents. In the end, of course, I was the loser.

While in Paris, I had unknowingly become addicted to wine and had hit a liter of wine a day. Except for kosher holiday wine, my parents never bought alcohol, nor did they serve it, but they had an extensive collection of liquor in the cellar, given to my father by grateful patients. I selected a fine bottle of Haig & Haig Scotch, smuggled it up to my ice blue tomb room, drank a bit less of it every day, and weaned myself from my alcohol addiction in under a month.

While I was in Europe, my Uncle Walter had died and I missed his funeral. Fortunately though, I had not missed my sister's wedding. She had married Andre just before I had left for Paris, her tasteful wedding accomplished in my parents' understated style in the backyard of our childhood home.

Just as at funerals one thinks about one's mortality, at weddings one thinks of one's own marriage, past or possible. But I did not. Although "wedding" was comprehensible to me, the phrase "*my* wedding" had no meaning for me. It never occurred to me that a woman would want to marry me. My socialization had never included the idea of growing up, of becoming a husband — let alone a father, of having a job, or of many other aspects of being an adult. This lack of or difference in socialization led me into many mistakes, which cost me an enormous investment of time, effort and understanding to make right. I must admit, however, that often my "self-repairs" were better than socialization by others.

Perhaps I was lucky in having escaped a more typical American adolescence. And no matter one's circumstances, there are always errors and painful mistakes. Under this heading, not marrying Shelly was one of my big ones. Shelly was young, dark and beautiful and we spent the summer of 1968

My sister Evy and her husband Andre. This photograph was taken around 2000.

together in New York. At the end of the summer, I said good-bye to her at the airport without ever having told her how I felt about her because it never occurred to me she might return the feeling. Not until years later did my friend Gene tell me that Shelly had wanted to marry me. My inability or refusal to express my feelings was such a needless cruelty. It would not be until my cancer that I would come to express all feelings and even to weep without embarrassment.

In the year of my absence, Berkeley had changed too. The politics had shifted from civil rights to anti-war. What was left of civil rights had largely become black power played out with a combination of heightened abstraction and increased violence. I heard Stokely Carmichael declaim from the steps of Sproul Hall that whites could best contribute to blacks by attending to white society. As always, I was overly sensitive to rejection. Viet Nam, however, did not remain abstract long. The possibility of being drafted permeated the consciousness of every male student at Cal but I took my 4-F status so for granted that I never registered for the draft.

As Yale had given way to Berkeley, so too now folk music gave way to rock. San Francisco was something of a center for rock. Local talent like the Jefferson Airplane, Janis Joplin and Big Brother and the Holding Company, Country Joe and the Fish, and other glory upon glory shared the stage at Bill Graham's Fillmore Auditorium with groups from across the country — even James Brown, whom I had loved as a teenager along with Bach, Bird, and Bartok.

I discovered three things: I liked the music. People danced to it. (How could you dance to Joan Baez?) And I could indeed dance. With the proper mixture of grass and booze I could dance damn well. In those days when whites were just learning to dance there were many styles they had from the folk style of white dancing, through modern dance and jazz dance, to the screw style where dance was by way of a public version of sex. My style was eclectic and informed by my movement disorder, dystonia. I learned how to turn the motions of my disability into the movements of dance. At times, particularly before whites learned to dance, my dance was dazzling. I had developed a social grace. I danced not only at the Fillmore but also at clubs like Steppenwolf in Berkeley and the Wildside in Oakland where white and black integrated in the jukebox and where I often danced with a tall black woman who turned out to be a transvestite.

Around this time, I became good friends with an easygoing law student named Mike Entin who was everything that I was not. Mike drove a car, flew a plane, effortlessly injected himself into social situations and was not involved in politics. A couple of times a week, Mike and I went to the Wildside nightclub. When Davida, my friend from Paris, showed up in Berkeley, Davida and I, along with Mike and his woman of the moment, drove to Oakland for nights of dancing. Soon Mike would become friends with Charlie Reich and be an inspiration for Charlie's book, *The Greening of America*. Two years later, Mike's plane would tragically crash into the Hollywood hills, and he would be gone.

After less than a week back in Berkeley I discovered another radical change in the political climate. I asked a woman friend to go with me to a movie and we each bought our own ticket. When I opened the theater door and waited for her to sail through, she asked, "What are you waiting for?"

"For you to go through the door."

"Why did you open the door?"

"For you."

"But you opened it. Why don't you go through?"

"I'm waiting for you."

"Why?"

I suppose I could have said "Why not?" and we could have gone on like that forever, but aside from being dumb, the conversation had become prickly. Yet, the more I thought about it, the less reason there was for me to stand there, door in hand.

And so it was that I walked awkwardly through the door of the women's movement. While I had been in Europe, movement women had grown tired of stuffing envelopes while the men planned demonstrations. They had gotten themselves together into an increasingly coherent women's movement with its own ideology, method, and perspective. The more I heard, the more reasonable it seemed. I did not then suspect the beneficial effects the movement would eventually have on me, a disabled man. Nor did I foresee that fifteen years later, back in New Haven on the staff of the Carnegie Council on Children, I would find myself part of a women's group at which time I would rethink the women's movement and pursue its relationship to children and to disability.

My initial reflections were more gut. I marveled that I had ignored an issue so close, this even after having read Simone de Beauvoir's *The Second Sex* while an undergraduate. But it would be many years until I reckoned the profound similarity of the women's movement to the disability rights movement. In the months that followed, I experienced and reflected on the effects of women's consciousness on me as a disabled man. My reflections were long and difficult. Macho was beyond me, or so I felt. Women had become more assertive and it seemed that life should become easier for me as a result. In some ways, I think it did. I no longer had to always initiate a relationship with women who found initiating as easy as opening doors. Although the women's movement helped me enormously, and I may owe my life with women to the movement, still it wasn't easy.

When I resumed classes at Berkeley again in the fall of 1966, I debriefed myself to the elfin Dean Elberg who chortled as I told him of my adventurous year in and out of Paris. Clearly satisfied that his money had been well spent, he closed our interview by advising me not to allow myself to be seduced by jobs — the thought had never occurred to me — and to go full tilt for my Ph.D.

To a shocking degree, and to an extent that was detrimental to any academic career, I treated graduate school as I had college. In general, I took the courses most interesting to me throughout the university. I had no conception of myself as an apprentice and hence would not become a journeyman. I missed out on many of the steps requisite to becoming an academic out of sheer ignorance of their existence.

At the time, I was studying international relations with Ernie Haas who misused mathematics in a style as prevalent to political science then as now. Bluntly, political science is not a science, and any use of mathematics except statistics is pretentious hubris. I called him on it every time, and soon he hated me. So when the then unknown Noam Chomsky who used mathematics properly and creatively was visiting Berkeley, I started cutting Ernie Haas's lectures in international relations in order to audit Chomsky's lectures in linguistics. When Ernie kicked me out of his class, I knew I would never be allowed to pass my qualifying exam in this field. Halfway through the semester I approached Herb McClosky who let me enter his political behavior class and who gave me even odds I might pass his course. I did.

Leaving international relations was a shame; it was one of several careers nipped in the bud. I'd always had a flair for it since my meeting as an undergraduate with George Kennan. While still a freshman in Brad Westerfield's course in international relations, I had read with horror Henry Kissinger's book *Nuclear Weapons and Foreign Policy* and had designed a nuclear deterrence policy, which was later adopted by the United States.

But now our involvement in Viet Nam was a more immediate question in foreign policy. At the beginning, I simply echoed the elite thinking of my undergraduate days. It took me months to reckon that we had no business in Viet Nam. The reckoning reached, I joined the anti-war movement.

During the old civil rights days of the early '60s, Berkeley students had raised demonstration to an art. Now I missed those days of moral clarity. Joining the anti-war movement required a leap of faith, fear, or thought. Since faith and fear were not options for me, thought was clearly my only choice. My brain made it impossible for me to do anything but join and the years that followed constituted an era of action, discussion and debate.

Throughout the years of the war, Berkeley became an obligatory campaign stop for people in the anti-war movement and Plato and Rousseau were routinely appealed to in speeches from the steps of Sproul Hall. One afternoon Noam Chomsky mounted the steps in front of Sproul Hall to argue the case for stopping the bombing in Viet Nam. His Cambridge orthodoxy drew scorn; Berkeley politicos favored an immediate insistence on withdrawal.

As student marches began to receive national press coverage, I was interviewed many times. One quote about the injustice of the war appeared in *Newsweek* as I discovered later when I received a piece of hate mail ending with this tender observation: "Your kind always dies." The note came in a large manila envelope that contained another already opened envelope addressed simply to William Roth, University of California. This letter had first gone to another William Roth who was on the Board of Regents of the University of California. So it was that I learned that privacy was never guaranteed, that I was not the only William Roth in the world, and that I should only tell reporters exactly what I wanted printed.

Came the spring of 1967 and Cal blossomed in vegetation. The skies glowed a freshly clear blue. The campus was thick with sexuality and I had my first experience in what pop sociology then called serial monogamy. My first girlfriend's wealthy father gave her a brand new silver blue Thunderbird for her birthday. I swallowed the bohemian pride that did not allow for pretentious Thunderbirds and went along for a three-month ride.

Spring also brought with it the renewal of political engagement. At times I was part of the planning for the spring demonstration; at other times I was a spectator. I did my part although my disability interfered with and even influenced my political activity. Because of my movement disorder, the stakes of marching in a demonstration were higher. I could not survive many demonstrations like the one I had survived in Greece. I could not depend on myself to be able to run to save myself. Because of my brain surgeries, I could not afford to get hit on the head. In addition, many of my compatriots did not want me in situations of violence. As a result, my disability sidelined me from critical parts of the important political struggle I was passionately invested in. This marginalization distressed me.

During the summer of '68, I took a course in filmmaking at San Francisco State University during which I made a film loosely based on Michelle, the woman who lived upstairs from Moe's bookstore. The experience taught me not only how to make films but also that I was good at it. I went on to make other films including *Long After Viet Nam* in which Don Duncan, an ex-green beret, played a character much like himself remembering his relationship with a Vietnamese woman. Although clumsy, it was coherent, and the film impresses me more now than when I made it. My involvement in politics and film led to my teaching an experimental course at Cal on the subject and to the topic of my Ph.D. dissertation, *Technology, Film, and the Body Politic.* It also led me to be a film critic for *Rolling Stone* magazine, and to design and teach courses on film history, filmmaking, and politics and film.

As U.S. involvement in the war grew more fierce, so too did the campus political activities. Soon the National Guard beefed up the ranks of police. Helicopters discharged tear and pepper gas. The students perfected the skill of throwing back tear gas canisters, talking to the National Guardsmen between engagements, and holding press conferences. I became more and more involved in the anti-war movement and discovered that I handled myself calmly and intelligently in chaotic and dangerous situations.

By the spring of 1969 Cal had reached such a state of anti-war sophistication that events that could have made other universities close down led Cal to form an alternative university where alternative classes were taught by university faculty at off-campus locations. The idea of alternatives expanded when people from all walks of life took over a vacant university lot and turned it into the glorious People's Park whose construction created solidarity and community. As People's Park was threatened with being shut down and bulldozed flat, thousands gathered to protest. The protests turned into riots when some protesters threw rocks and metal rods at the police. Governor Ronald Reagan ordered 2,000 National Guardsmen in full battle gear to put down the protests.

At five o'clock on the morning of the march, I was up editing my film, *Long After Viet Nam,* when I saw the police and National Guard in black battle jackets stationed on the buildings along the route of the march. For many days, Berkeley streets were shrouded in a blanket of tear gas. In the weeks that followed, the Guard kept up an armed presence. In the end, many people were injured, and later reports say one was blinded, and another was shot and killed. I never forgave Ronald Reagan for the gratuitous show of force that led to unnecessary death.

To pursue my formal education for a doctorate, at first I had pure fellowships. Later I had teaching assistantships, first in political theory, later one in architecture. I then developed and taught an experimental course in politics and film. Subsequently I taught politics and art for a year in the humanities program at the San Francisco Art Institute. I had known artists before, but this was my first sustained contact with them. I came to admire the people who dared to make art instead of war. I learned as I taught, from preparation, from what I taught, from whom I taught.

In the fall of the academic year 1969–1970, while finishing my dissertation, I co-taught with Peter Selz a graduate course in the Art History Department titled *Twentieth Century Art and Politics.* Teaching art historians, most of whom actually seemed to dislike art, was very different from teaching undergraduates or artists. Reluctantly, I concluded that most art historians dislike art and try to talk or speak to the impossible and to categorize to give the delusion of comprehension. The main intellectual tool of art historians then was "influence" as in "Picasso was influenced by African art." This comprehension by influence struck even me, a budding social scientist, as naive.

Peter was a curator of the Berkeley Art Museum, which had just moved into a spanking new building. I conceived and organized an exhibition slated to open in time for Mother's Day in which women would be chained to major household appliances — washing machine, stove, etc. Peter liked the idea so much he proposed that it be the opening exhibit for the new museum. As I began to publicize the exhibit, women formed themselves into opposing groups, those in support of the show and those against. Although my intention was *for* the Women's Movement, I was happy to help organize the pickets on both sides. On May 4, 1970, the week the show would have opened, National Guardsmen shot and killed four students at Kent State University. When I heard the news, I canceled the show and it became an undocumented piece of conceptual art.

Although conceptual art had been cancelled, love had not. *Twentieth Century Art and Politics* went well, and there I met Moira, my first wife, when she danced into the class to give Peter a draft of her dissertation. She was British and possessed an unusual charm and charisma. And although she mockingly referred to the Queen as "Queenie," she was herself a princess. And unlike many art historians, she actually loved art and life. Moira was a thoroughly decent woman who later once described our marriage as reckless. Perhaps she referred to my immaturity and to my utter lack of social preparation for marriage.

But prepared or not, time goes on and so did I. In the spring of 1970 I received my Ph.D. in Political Science from Berkeley. Moira and I left for Los Angeles where she had found a university job. After a couple of years of following her around the country from university to university where I was unable to find work, I took a job at the University of Vermont where in rapid succession I got myself arrested, jailed, fired and divorced.

But I am ahead of myself. When I left Berkeley, I had just turned thirty and although not grown up, I was on my way. I was well educated, well traveled, and married. I had played an active role in an historic movement and had been actively aware and engaged at a political crosshairs of place and time. I'm honored to have been at Berkeley in the '60s and carry the generous gifts of that time and place into the life I live today.

CHAPTER 23

A Radical Reunion,
Spring 1989

During my long months of chemotherapy, Daniel and I continued our custom of weekly dinners out. But now the radius of restaurants that I was able to reach by walking shrank from the splendors of greater downtown Albany to the closer pleasures of the neighborhood P. D. Ladd's, two-and-a-half blocks away. For me, this was fine; eating was not the pleasure it had once been and this gave me more time to focus on Daniel. During one such dinner in the middle of winter, when the snow had turned from white to a grey soup of slush and frozen garbage, Daniel said, "One of my friends said you're going to die."

I froze mid-chew, my molars about to grind an overcooked carrot. I froze not because the thought had not crossed my mind, but because someone had actually spoken the thought to Daniel. I had foolishly assumed that Daniel would only know what his family told him or what he guessed.

"Who did you hear that from?" I asked.

"From David," answered Daniel.

David was the son of the Hudson family down the street who had just lost their daughter, Melina, in Pan Am Flight 103 over Lockerbie, Scotland, and at whose memorial service I had wept.

"Where do you think David heard it?" I asked.

"His mother," said Daniel. "She said you were going to die."

"What do you think?" I asked.

"I don't know," said Daniel.

Matters had escalated. My death was now a topic of conversation for Daniel's friends. He was living in his own culture and open to its influences. The matter of my death had to be engaged at a more serious, formidable level. But I could not talk with Daniel about the probability of my death. As Solnit had told me earlier, ten-year-olds do not know what to make of probabilities.

I looked Daniel clean in the eye and asked rhetorically, "Am I going to die?" Then I answered my own question. "No. I am not going to die."

I took a breath and moved into deeper waters perhaps over my head. As I spoke, my commitment to fight for my life strengthened. "But I will make you a promise. If I'm ever going to die, I will be the first to tell you."

This promise changed my relationship to Daniel from one of protection to one of honesty. Daniel seemed satisfied. I was a bit overwhelmed but ultimately satisfied too.

With my disability, falling is a common event for me which is why, when I fall, I fall masterfully. My feet do not rise much above the ground; rather, they hug it. Therefore, I wear out the soles of my shoes unevenly and lickety split, and frequently stumble and sometimes trip. At its extreme, my disability imposes unpredictable lurches and stumbles on my walking gait. Since adolescence when my spine had keeled over and I walked apelike, my hands swinging just over the ground, I'd regarded the ground as a friend. Like Antaeus, I draw strength from it. But despite my mastery, I sometimes tear my pants, scrape my hands or knees, and have even demolished several watches. I used to get angry once. No longer. Falling, although not quite an everyday event, is a common and acceptable cost of doing business.

Now I took a nasty fall. No bother. I tore the hand that broke the fall and gashed the skin above my right kneecap that took the brunt of the fall. I bled heavily for a while and accepted the destruction of my pants. But this fall had different consequences. The gash took weeks to heal. The chemotherapy that kills rapidly multiplying cancer cells also kills the growing cells that heal wounds.

During the course of chemotherapy, I received many wounds that took unnerving lengths of time to heal. This vulnerability shook me. When I finally reached the end of twenty-one courses of chemotherapy, DeConti proposed that since I was reacting well to the chemotherapy, and that since the exact number of courses had not been established in the literature, it was only logical to continue.

Logic against my wishes, I continued. But within a couple of weeks of this decision, a pain developed toward the base of my tongue. Like other cancer patients, I suffered an unspeakable fear of symptoms that an ordinary person would ignore. This fear is not related to anxiety, guilt, worry, or any other irrational neurosis. This fear is altogether sensible, logical, and rational with cancer.

Although it was a Sunday, I tracked DeConti down at the hospital and, at his request, met him at the Emergency Room. There, despite a thorough examination of the inside of my mouth, he could find nothing. DeConti suggested that I see Parnes that Monday. As Parnes was out of town, I made an appointment with a young assistant. After an extensive search he found a spot visible only in his laryngoscope. He said that he wanted to take a biopsy. With any other person the spot could safely be regarded as just a plain old sore. With a cancer patient little can be taken for granted. He gave me a local anesthetic and took a small punch biopsy. Ordinarily the biopsy wound would have healed in a short time. With chemotherapy it was not about to heal.

I spent the next two days after the biopsy locked in the primitive fear reserved for one stalked by a murderer. To my relief, the biopsy came back negative. But the sore still wouldn't heal. Sasaki called the lesion a response to radiation. One side effect of methotrexate is mucositis, an erosion of the mucous membranes. Fisher and DeConti decided that my chemotherapy had to be stopped.

It was spring again. I had been at war for a year. We had used almost every weapon in the arsenal of cancer medicine. Now I lived defenseless and without a bodyguard. I was naked.

Less than a month after stopping chemo, at my monthly appointment with Parnes, he ordered a CAT scan that showed a mass under my left jawbone about three centimeters — a little more than an inch — in diameter. The imaging radiologist in Albany called the mass "highly suspicious."

If the lesion in my mouth had frightened me, now I was terrified. I split into two people and immediately got on my case. I gave Sasaki's nurse, Paulette, a call and asked her to squeeze me in. I grabbed the CAT scan, my friend Rick drove me down to New Haven, and my mother met me at Sasaki's office. Sasaki took a look at the scan and saw where the bump was. His marvelous fingers carefully felt my neck. He appeared puzzled. Cancer has a characteristic hard feel to it. He could not feel anything and he preferred clinical judgment over technology. But cancer does not yield to preference. It is obnoxious that way.

Sasaki was a man of few words, which gave the words he did say a particular weight. "I'm going to set up a needle biopsy under CAT scan," he said. "I can't feel anything, but there is something in the scan." When the door shut behind Sasaki, I burst into tears, not from fear, but from the sudden relief of coming back together — of two adding back up to one again — and the relief of having the terrible verdict of the CAT scan contradicted by Sasaki's fingers and his clinical judgment.

Hearing my weeping, Paulette walked in and wrapped her arms around me in the hug of a woman. She had the good sense not to ask what the matter was. She just hugged me and stroked my head while I cried, exactly what I desperately needed at the exact right moment.

The biopsy and the CAT scan were scheduled in six days. Once again I settled my affairs, which were already in very good order from so much settling, and then waited. The following Wednesday, I showed up for the biopsy appropriately sedated. I knew that I would have to be perfectly still for the scan and had asked Lew to call the imaging radiologist to arrange to use the appropriate narcosis. Otherwise, the sudden movements of my dystonia might interfere with the delicate procedure.

I had gotten so good at discussing the fine points of my medical procedures that the radiologist asked, "Are you a physician?"

"Only as a hobby," I joked.

"I wish my students were as good as you," he said.

But really, I was cheating. I had come full circle. The stereotaxic procedures the radiologist would use were in principle the same procedures I had undergone with Cooper during my late teens.

The radiologist established the reference points, attached a guide, and the needle vectored inward. Every two millimeters the CAT scan checked the needle's position. The procedure took several hours, twice as long as it should have, because despite being well drugged, my body still moved. Each milligram of tranquilizer, narcotic and anesthetic was matched with a milligram of fear, dread, and panic. At the end of the procedure, loaded with enough drugs to knock out a horse, I popped up and walked right out with my mother.

I knew enough about needle biopsies to know that preliminary results would be available that same afternoon. I telephoned the radiologist and asked for the preliminary results. They showed nothing, and a rush of relief coursed through me.

The next morning, Thursday, was the day of my twenty-fifth Yale reunion. The reunion had long been a bright spot on my clouded horizon, and I was eager to go. The first event, my Senior Society dinner party, would be held that evening. When I called Sasaki's office to confirm the results of the biopsy, he said, "The results of the needle biopsy are positive. Come on in. We need to talk."

Somewhat dazed, I arrived at his office where he outlined the game plan. First, a radical neck dissection followed by an excision of the tumor and the implantation of radioactive seeds along the margins of the tumor. He had an opening on his surgical calendar in three weeks.

Stunned, I shifted gears and divided in two. This odd splitting was automatic and fully integrated into my operating system. My situation was serious, but I did not recognize how serious. I still thought there was perhaps about a five percent chance of winning. In truth, with my history, a recurrence of the cancer was almost the same as a death sentence.

In rapid sequence, I went to see Lew who called his friend, the very same physician who had been head of the Yale health service when my acceptance to Yale had been questioned. He called an expert in head and neck cancer in another city who agreed with Sasaki's proposal. I would discover later that Lew called Sasaki to make a case for excision of the tumor and a frozen section. Sasaki said that was unacceptable surgical practice. If the tumor were excised first, the chances for a successful radical neck would be compromised.

Clearly my situation was grave. Placing radioactive seeds into an area that had already received its fill of radiation was dangerous. From Lew's office I called Solnit, who made time for me at five o'clock, and Gary whom I arranged to meet on Friday morning at our class reunion.

A short while later at Solnit's office, I cried briefly, and explained what had happened. Although he knew I wanted to talk about other things, Solnit would not leave the topic of the surgery. This was unlike him. Yet he pressed each point. When was the CAT scan taken? What had the biopsy shown? Was the radiation necessary? Then he said, "Until now you have weathered all the procedures remarkably well. You have to be sure you need these new procedures. Get a second opinion."

I was dumbfounded. Not only was Solnit toying in an area where I needed him least, he was also putting my ability to organize the team into question. Why was he doing this? When I got back to my mother's house, I called Rick and explained to him what happened. "Solnit really threw me," I said. "He grilled me on purpose and that threw me even more." After talking it through, we concluded that Solnit had taken a calculated risk. He wanted me to be absolutely sure about the radical neck and the radiation. He trusted my strength enough to risk upsetting me at a critical point. That suspicion seemed right to both of us.

Still reeling from my death sentence, I headed out to my Senior Society's dinner party. The whole idea of being at a party while death was pounding on my door was illogical. I tried.

At the party, I connected myself back together, two back to one. I found myself tired, outspoken, and loving. I enjoyed the successes of the other members of my Senior Society and was interested in the trajectories that had led one to have a second wife, another to have a large family, another to be childless, another to be very successful, another to be successful, another to be happy, another to be grumpy, et cetera.

Most of my classmates were in very good shape for their age, characteristic for graduates of an Ivy League school. For them death was only a hint of mortality and old age. Almost at the heights of their careers and vectored upward, they were concerned with success while I was concerned with the grave.

"Hey Bill, you want something to eat?" Michael Batten, now a corporate CEO, was standing in front of me, offering to fill my plate. My mouth was exquisitely dry. "Yes, thanks," I said. "Everything on the plate has to be moist or greasy." Then I explained that dry food and a dry mouth do not go together.

Gradually the thirty people in the room came to know that I had cancer. Most people walked over to talk with me. Some avoided me. No one, including me, knew how serious it was. No one was insane enough to give me advice.

Tiredness fought with my pleasure in the reunion until finally tiredness won out. Will Elting, now a Texas oilman, offered to take me home. He still had the powerful body of the varsity rower he had once been. I had always liked Will. He had been to my house as an undergraduate and now he drove me to my mother's house.

Yale is known for alumni loyalty. This is not due to public relations, but to the years during which undergraduates receive the best resources that the university has to offer. For example, Yale's best professors teach the introductory courses. Undergraduate Yalies are coddled, nurtured, excited, and led to feel better than the students at the university's many graduate and professional schools.

The next day at the Old Campus, a huge courtyard framed by the freshman dormitories, I sat in the class of '64 tent. Dennis DeSilvey, now a cardiologist and a member of my Senior Society, joined me. Dennis knew little of my cancer, and I knew nothing about his abilities as a physician. I told him that a physician had suggested that I get a second opinion. The discussion that proceeded was not exactly relevant to my case. Yet merely talking made me feel more comfortable, alert, and mobilized.

Other people stopped by my corner of the tent. Who should I tell that I had cancer? Who should I not tell? Cancer was not the whole of my life. I was proud of my life and felt like talking about other parts of it. Some people I told. Others I did not. I do not know why.

A tall, slender figure with black curly hair appeared on the other side of the tent. Gary. As if in a dream, I called to him but could not make my soft, post-radiation voice heard. Slowly, clumsily, I began to scramble after him still calling. He was ambling slowly. Finally, he heard me, and we hugged. Knowing that he would understand, I looked into his loving eyes and said, "I need to talk to you."

Gary and I went for lunch. With friends greeting us seemingly at every moment, we finally found a bit of uninterrupted space and time. I laid it all out for him: the positive biopsy, Solnit's questions, and my own doubts. Gary already knew the possible consequences of a radical neck dissection. As we talked, my course became clear.

After lunch at Yale, I called Lew who cleared an hour for me. Once facing him in his office, I expressed my doubts about having the radical. He put me on the phone to his oncologist friend whom he had already thoroughly briefed. The friend had called a national expert and was satisfied that a radical was in order. He gave me the name of the expert, and I gave her a call. By the end I was satisfied. That evening I called Solnit at his home, told him what I had done and asked him if he thought it constituted a second opinion. He asked questions, and said that it did. Finally I asked, "Why did you insist on spending so much time talking medicine when you knew it would upset me? Why did you question the judgment of people on whom I had come to rely?"

"It was a calculated risk. I thought you could handle it."

We both knew that I had handled it and was better for having done so.

Meanwhile, Judith and Daniel arrived at my mother's house to accompany me the next day to the reunion picnic. The next day the three of us went to a country club near New Haven where the Class of 1964 was holding its reunion picnic. By this time, Judith and I had become painfully distant — a distance I experienced as icy coldness on her part. Yet, despite the difficulties between us, with her lovely hair and lithe figure, Judith was absolutely beautiful, and I was proud of her and proud of Daniel too.

The food was sumptuous, the athletic facilities grand, but what impressed Daniel most was a Good Humor ice cream truck that gave away free popsicles.

What impressed me most was a softball game in which Daniel was catcher. A large pot-bellied member of the class of '64 ran from third to home. The ball was thrown to the catcher. The man slammed into Daniel. Daniel was shaken up, but okay. The man was out. Utterly unfazed, Daniel prepared for the next play. An intangible yet definite toughness had entered Daniel since the year before. I was so proud of him — and relieved. He might need the toughness.

Determined to savor what might be my last reunion, I spent most of the afternoon tired, sitting at a table, and enjoying the friends who stopped to talk. I stayed well beyond the point of exhaustion. Matters of life and death had absorbed the first day of my reunion. I would not lose out on this day.

That weekend, my cousin Ernie arranged a dinner at one of New Haven's many exceptional Italian restaurants to celebrate my 47th birthday. What was left of my family surrounded me at the table. Judith and Daniel were there, as were my mother, my sister, Evy, her husband, Andre, and her daughter,

Simone. My cousin Ernie and his wife, Helene, and their sons, Mark and Glenn, were also there, as was my cousin Diane and her husband, Robert. Even my Aunt Hertha was there, her breast cancer seemingly under control.

When they sang "Happy Birthday, Dear Billy," the older generation, unable to pronounce the "th" in birthday, singing instead "birszday," I left the table, faded over to a corner, and wept.

CHAPTER 24

A Nice Guy Like Me,
1970–1978

On many sleepless cancer nights I reviewed my past, replaying my history like a film scholar replaying a film. Here's Bill, 47-year-old professor, father of Daniel, with a wife who won't sleep with him let alone drive him to his cancer appointments, watching part of his life's work go down in flames, living in Albany, New York, staring at the ceiling of his home office from his bed on the floor, asking himself, "What's a nice guy like me doing in a place like this?"

It's a long story. After graduating from Berkeley in 1970, I spent a year with my first wife Moira in Los Angeles where I discovered that, according to a state vocational rehabilitation assessment, I did not qualify for sweeping floors. Although I did qualify for teaching, at the time there were still strict rules against nepotism and my odds of getting a job in the same town as my wife were almost nil. I had taken a job at Dartmouth College in 1971 teaching a course on Buster Keaton, a hero of mine, when my friend Rick Sugarman invited me to the University of Vermont to interview for a job. My interview was a smash, and I received an appointment for the 1971–72 academic year in the University of Vermont's Department of Political Science.

Until Vermont, I had never been arrested. But when the U.S. mined the harbor of Haiphong in May of 1972, the University of Vermont held the largest demonstration in the country. As momentum for the demonstration increased, the chances of it ending in violence increased. As I reviewed the cast of characters, I saw that no one except me had been schooled in the art of demonstration. Having come of age in Berkeley, I was fully experienced with demonstrations and knew that these students of Vermont did not have the discipline for active resistance. They were novices, many of whom were inclined to do battle with the police. If left to their own devices, they might

131

well get hurt. The police were inexperienced at demonstrations as well. This had to be a peaceable sit-in.

Out of responsibility to the students, I decided to lead half of the demonstration around one door at the Federal Building. Around my entrance there was a cordon of young and frightened looking policemen twitched their long riot clubs. Had they been wealthier, they might have been students. Looking young and frightened, the students sat down. Had they been poor, they might have been policemen.

In times of danger, I am absolutely calm. "Stay right where you are," I instructed the students. "If the police come to arrest you, go limp and let them pick you up. Do not resist. Do not say anything."

Still calm, I limped out towards the line of policemen anxiously fingering their riot clubs. The chief of police came from behind the line and walked toward me. We met just in front of the line. "What do you want?" asked the chief.

"These students will not resist arrest if you send in police without clubs," I said.

"How can I believe that?" he said.

"Because I told you," I replied calmly. "What do you have to lose?"

"All right, go ahead," he answered. "I'll send my men over in groups of two."

I went back inside, dispatched one of the students to get a message to Rick to arrange for bail, and taught fifty students a quick lesson in non-violent resistance 101. Each student went limp in the arms of two policemen. No one was hurt. I had done my job as a teacher.

The chief of police came over to thank me.

I said, "Aren't you going to arrest me?"

"I don't want to," said the chief.

"I think you'd better," I said.

"O.K., if you insist."

I insisted. The door to the last vehicle was open and in I hobbled. I insisted because not only did these kids not know how to act in demonstrations, they also did not know how to act in jail. I wanted to be in a position to keep some sort of order in the jailhouse. As it turned out, a crazy faculty member and his gang devised a plan to storm the jail to free us. Nobody had a right to break us out if we didn't want it. From within, I issued the following declarative message: "Not until we get out."

Rick arranged bail and we were out the same day.

That evening, some 2,000 students assembled in Waterman Hall for a meeting, which everyone — including me — assumed I would lead. A few minutes before the meeting a delegation of kids walked up to me and said, "We appreciate everything you did today. Well, it just wouldn't look right to have a handicapped person lead the demonstration and be our spokesperson."

It wouldn't look good to have a crip at the head of their parade. The situation was too outrageous to merit argument. Angry and full of a corrosive pity, I said, "Sure. Go ahead. It's your show."

Several weeks later, with Rick acting as my lawyer, I pleaded *nolo contendre*— no contest — in front of a judge named Roth. My prosecutor was a young lawyer named Patrick Leahy who would later become a senator from Vermont.

We could easily have had a blood bath that day. Many years later after Vermont's other senator Bernie Sanders was elected mayor of Burlington I found out that during that crisis, five hundred inexperienced, fearful National Guardsmen with loaded rifles and extra ammunition had been hidden in the basement of City Hall. Fear is dangerous, armed fear doubly so.

Although this event occurred before I made the critical connections between civil rights, women's rights, the anti-war movement, and the rights of people with disabilities, I had made a critical connection between boyhood and manhood, between private and public self and between psychology and sociology.

At Monument Valley, in the 1990s.

During that very full year of light and dark at Vermont, I lived in a dormitory room above the practice room of a rock & roll band; my university friend, Dick Warner, died of cancer; and Rick and I had many conspiratorial conversations over martinis in the Black Cat Grill directed toward the governance of Burlington, Vermont. The possibilities in these conversations were realized and amplified by Rick in his association with Bernie Sanders when Bernie later became mayor of Burlington. Rick remained behind the scenes, one of the few philosophers to see his ideas put into action, theory into practice. I also taught a course on politics and the American Western which spun off presentations throughout the country and an article on politics and the western in the esoteric *Film Culture* magazine. In between cowboys and politicians, I joined an attempt to retain a tenured professor who had been fired for waving a North Vietnamese flag. The attempt failed and by the end of the year he was fired, and I found myself with a contract that was not renewed. The reasons, of course, were political. The consequences were profound. It is no casual matter for disabled people to lose a job; some three-quarters of us are out of work or underemployed. If worse comes to worse, the able-bodied can drive cabs or work in factories. I cannot. My disability made me unqualified to drive a cab, wait tables, or in fact do anything physical except dance, make love or arm wrestle.

After I was let go from my job, and with the idea that cross-country marriages were unworkable, I asked Moira, who was then in Los Angeles starting her splendid career as an art historian, for a divorce.

Before I got canned at the University of Vermont, I had interviewed for a job at Yale where my old mentor Ed Lindblom was chairman of the Political Science Department. I made my presentation on politics and film to the department. Not surprisingly, I did not get the job. However, one of the people present, Michael Lerner, was particularly impressed. Lerner was a friend of Kenneth Keniston, then at the summit of his reputation as an expert on youth, who would soon be charged with creating and directing the Carnegie Council on Children. I met Keniston at the then upscale Casey's restaurant in New Haven where he explained his conception of the council and conducted a most thorough and skillful job interview without ever saying that's what it was. Everything about it sounded exciting. I would have the chance to explore a new field and to contribute to significant policy recommendations.

When he offered me the job, Keniston told me that I had the capacity to make other people comfortable with my disability. I would have reason to remember this compliment later. But for now I was offered a job on the staff that exceeded anything I could have dreamt of. The Carnegie Council on

Children included people like Marion Wright Edelman, Patricia Wald, and Laura Nader. The staff included half a dozen young people, some of with whom I would become close friends. Ironically, none of us had children, but to balance that we were all young and presumably childlike.

As the Carnegie Council on Children was essentially an independent part of Yale University, I found myself back in New Haven at my alma mater. We were housed in a stately brick mansion at the top of Prospect Street, surely one of Yale's best locations, and our excellent administrative staff was culled from among the best Yale had to offer.

That first summer, I immersed myself with my colleagues in an intense study of children and found an apartment in downtown New Haven some two miles and a comfortable hour's walk from my parents' home. Inside Carnegie, I remained closest to Michael Lerner. Outside of Carnegie, I became friends with Catharine "Kitty" MacKinnon, a future celebrity radical feminist; John Gliedman, a brilliant psychologist with an encyclopedic breadth of knowledge who also shared my politics; and Samia Halaby, a profound Palestinian artist. All of these friendships had a remarkable effect on me.

The next year the politically talented Richard deLone was recruited to direct the staff. Had he not been stricken and taken by lymphoma, he would doubtless have become something like mayor of his beloved hometown, Philadelphia, or have had a position in the Clinton administration. Hillary Rodham with her raucous laugh also joined the staff. For the year she was with us, my $25 L.A. thrift store elephant skin Gladstone bag was a continual object of her laughter. She brought her boyfriend, Bill, to one of the many parties at the mansion to which I had also invited my parents. Bill sidled up to my father and a half hour later, my father reported to me, "That boy's going to be president."

Every couple of months, the Carnegie Council on Children met to focus on a different aspect of children. Each meeting was held in a different location from Cuernavaca to Cape Cod to San Diego to Berkeley. We on the staff participated in all the meetings.

If all this sounds like heady stuff, it was. And underlying the glamour was deep, meaningful, satisfying work that culminated in the publication of five books that laid out a progressive policy for America's children. However, America's later sharp cut to the right left the work of the Carnegie Council largely unrecognized and its policy recommendations untried. John Gliedman put it best when he said, "It was the last serious stand of liberalism in America."

During my second year at the Council, motivated by my own experience of disability and an ethical obligation to tackle an "orphan" subject, I volunteered to write a book on handicapped children. In typical Carnegie fashion, I set off to Washington, D.C., with tape recorder in hand to interview officials in the Nixon administration about public policy for disabled children. After a couple of days of talking to high-level officials about low-level children, my hackles were up. I had learned to trust myself enough to follow my discomfort to its source. These officials spoke about handicapped children as objects. Although severely disabled, as a child I had never been an object. Carnegie had taught me that those who talked of children as objects usually had other agendas. Most of the people in charge of programs and policy had Potomac fever, a grotesque insider's disease characterized by feelings of grandeur and power.

After several days in Washington, D.C., for which I conceived an intense dislike, I left for Willowbrook, a notorious institution in Staten Island, New York, for people with developmental disabilities. There I would spend two days that would change my life.

I arrived at Willowbrook on the first day of spring, in the time after Willowbrook became a media event but before it drifted into cultural amnesia. The lawns were fresh and green, the architecture gracious, spacious, and clean. Each cluster of red brick buildings housed hundreds of mentally retarded or developmentally disabled children, many of them now adults, who had been there for their entire lives. Outside, along the walkways under the trees, beneath the sun, there was no one.

I presented myself at the staff room of a new social service unit. These people were young, friendly, and enthusiastic. They joked over coffee and welcomed me, the outsider. Was this the Willowbrook about which I had read? Impossible. With people like this, what could be wrong?

The job of this social service unit was to place residents into the outside world. The section had an astonishingly high success rate of about fifty percent and the staff was justly proud. Then it occurred to me to ask, "What percentage does social service try to place?" The answer: less than one-half of one percent.

One of the women at the table offered to show me around. Maria was totally without pretension, direct, simple, sensuous, and loving. Her gestures quite naturally included touching me. She seemed to come from an entirely different culture. It turned out that she had. Leaving the building, she said, "You know, I used to be a resident here."

I did not believe her. It would take long reflection on the experiences of the whole day to comprehend that statement, "You know, I used to be a resident here."

Maria was bilingual. She spoke both English and Willowbrook. By

Willowbrook I refer not only to the institution, but also to its language, customs and culture. Throughout the day Maria interpreted the Willowbrook language of hugs and tone that evoked in me childhood associations. Without her I would not have understood what I witnessed that day.

I followed Maria outside to a big new children's building that she was proud of. Outside it was sunny, breezy and green. No children played on the big, beautiful, empty lawn. Inside the building, Maria had work to do, records to check and files to pull, and she left me on my own. Television sets were everywhere. Television watching, or a blank non-watching was, next to sleeping, the chief out-of-class activity of children. Television and drugs, pacification and power; both short-circuit the body and dominate the brain.

A trail of television sets led me to a classroom where the children hugged me. The classroom was elaborately decorated with simple cut out pictures drawn by the teacher. I tried to be an inconspicuous observer, but that was impossible because the children refused to not notice me. About a third of the children in the class had Down's syndrome, or Mongolism; we have no human word for it. Others were retarded or different in other ways. Others, to my eye, should not have been there.

The current lesson was on telling time. The teacher explained that because the children had very short attention spans, lessons were broken up into five-minute intervals. Some of the children followed the lesson. Most did not. Some were not even aware a lesson had occurred. The next lesson was letter bingo. The winners won a lollipop. I have never been a big fan of behavior modification in its disguise of humane control and cultured domination.

Without a context, a child with Down's syndrome is a clinical being defined by a syndrome. When we think of our brothers and sisters, they are brothers and sisters because they exist in a context of our situations and our histories, our homes and our families. But in an institution, it's hard to think of a human being as a human being because the context and nature of the institution is designed around their difference and domination and built to wall out empathy as it walls in people.

And Willowbrook was exquisite in its domination.

"What do they do after lunch?" I asked the teacher.

"They sit and watch television."

"They don't play with each other, they don't go outside?" I was shocked at their isolation from childhood.

"No. The outside is for *you* to look at when you come in. It's not for the children. If they go outside, they go out usually into playpens."

I asked, "What happens during the rest of the day?"

"The kids eat dinner. Then they sit —"

"They what?"

"They sit." What kid sits? Kids bounce, dash, and turn their bodies.

"Oh."

"Then they go to bed."

Now I understood that the only life with growth at Willowbrook — the only life that even remotely resembled what we ordinarily consider a life — occurred here in this classroom. Everywhere else was power and its assistants: difference, subjugation, domination, surveillance, et cetera.

Later that day, I followed Maria to a building reputed to be one of the worst where the violent young women lived, if "lived" is the right word; the same building where Maria was kept for five years. Despite her many years there, I saw nothing violent or antisocial in Maria's behavior.

Dr. Boswell was our guide for this part of the tour. We entered the building. Young women looking much older than their years and dressed in bizarre outfits moved aimlessly about. Some walked up the stairs. Some walked down the stairs. Some crawled up the stairs. Some crawled down the stairs. Some sat. For the first of many times that day and in days to follow, I wondered *how had Maria survived?*

Dr. Boswell opened a door into a bare room with some thirty-five indestructible fiberglass and steel chairs arranged in a circle. Women who sat like catatonics occupied ten of the chairs.

"Do you have many catatonics here?" I asked.

"These women aren't catatonics. They just learn that if you're going to sit in a chair all day, the best way of doing that is to sit with your legs all scrunched up. It takes less energy and is much more efficient."

Domination leads to submission not only abstractly, but also concretely in the body. The actions, language, and customs of these women were not warped or primitive, but rational expressions of their culture. The Willowbrook institutional culture machine dominates, dehumanizes, brutalizes, oppresses and objectifies. Drugged and constrained to inaction, the residents suffer an environmentally induced catatonia. The machine prescribes, dictates, and forces nothingness, and they have become masters of nothingness. The political and social environments have become tyrannical oppressors.

As an experiment, four women were allowed together in a room previously reserved for solitary confinement. Maria had spent many months in solitary in that same room. Although someone needed help badly, there was no attendant.

One woman was lying very still pressed naked against the floor. She had been lying on the floor longer than anyone could remember. No one was able to talk to her. She could not commit suicide even if her life was unbearable.

The water fountains were broken and the women drank from unflushed toilets. Many of the women crawled to make it easier to drink out of the toilet. The doctor flushed all the toilets knowing that it would not really make any difference. And it was the same in the next ward, the next ward, and the ward after.

Maria, as she would tell me later, felt deeply at seeing old friends and returning to the building that had hurt her. Later I would wonder: How had Maria survived? Why was she still beautiful? How had she come to be in Willowbrook in the first place? But for now all I could see was the quiet and efficient violence of the Willowbrook machine. Which makes even more curious and compelling the humanity of the Willowbrook residents and their special language. At Willowbrook everybody hugs you. Everybody gets hugged. Maria answered in Willowbrook, returning hug for hug, slapping the hand that went after her watch, but always slapping toward her, never rejecting the human bodies connected to the hands. Maria responded appropriately to a language that threatened me. In so doing, she made Willowbrook's language and society comprehensible to me.

From watching Maria, it was easy to learn at least the rudiments of how to lift someone's hands from you, how to let somebody hug you. I learned that, as bizarre as they looked, the people around me were people. But like inmates and slaves they were people who had been powerfully socialized.

Power over time can lead to bizarre socialization. The system starts with disabled children — lively children, obviously human, who enjoy life. Over time, these children grow into adults who sit in chairs all day long rocking back and forth. Trained by power to be docile, depressed, and submissive, their minds are now warped and rotted far beyond the initial infirmity that they arrived with. First, there is the wound; Down's syndrome, cerebral palsy, hyperactivity, mental retardation, mislabeling, et cetera, then there is the salt — Willowbrook. This training and response to passivity is only efficient and humane because it dispenses with the need for continual violence, direction, and supervision. What is true for the children is only somewhat less true for the staff.

The staff is also institutionalized. The longer the patient has been in the system, the more rigid and brutal the staff become. They exploit the power relationships between them and the residents. These attendants are unionized, and the union is not about to have any of them fired. The residents have no union.

Willowbrook thrives on marginality. We build Willowbrooks and then staff them with marginalized people, many of whom are also somehow different. Marginal people can be controlled and dominated more efficiently and more cost-effectively. We pack them — the residents and the staff — all together and they effectively "neutralize" each other while creating a layer of insulation between the institutionalized *them* and the outside *us*. And we do not really care as long as we do not have to hear or see them.

I did not then think of myself as one of them. I did notice, however, that I introduced myself as Dr. Roth and that I connected myself unduly and unusually to Carnegie and Yale. Although comfortable with myself psychologically, I still had to develop a social and political conception of myself as a disabled person. I did not yet appreciate that some others might conceive of me as a disabled outsider.

Contagion is compelling. The plague, syphilis, peer influence, "cooties," leprosy, et cetera, echo through history. The germ theory runs wild with ethnic cleansing and genocide. Contagion is meant to apply precisely to those things we wish to isolate and destroy. In the name of such, quarantine, asepsis, and antisepsis is not only permissible but also necessary.

Contagion, germs, institution, bodies, et cetera, boil in a soup of power. "Don't play with the Jones boy. He is a bad influence." We learn not to play with the Jones boy. We may be afraid of catching blackness, so African Americans are put in a ghetto where they will not infect us. We are afraid of catching mental illness, so we keep mentally ill people at a safe distance. Old age may sneak in through the back door, so we lock the door and turn on the television.

Which led me to a dilemma. Should I wash my hands, or should I not wash my hands before eating? My hands were sticky from touching so many other sticky hands. All manner of infectious disease could have been exchanged in the hugs and handshaking of the morning. If I washed my hands, I would be admitting my "outsiderness" and their "otherness." I feared catching something dreadful. Call it Willowbrook disease. For the first time in my life, washing or not washing my hands became a political decision. I ended up washing my hands, assuring myself I was not attempting to wash away responsibility but simply washing my hands because they needed washing.

Later, I met with Arthur, an outside expert on child welfare. He wanted to visit some children's buildings and I went along with him outside again into the warm, green, desolate spring. Back inside, we met a boy with spina bifida and a little girl in a wheelchair, nasty Alice, who pestered him sexually. Nearby was a bed with a teddy bear in it. No. Not a teddy bear but a tiny child propped up and entirely motionless. On another bed, a boy rocked back and forth. In a play area with three children and no toys, one little boy sat on the floor rocking back and forth, another sat on the floor doing nothing and a third wandered in precise circles. Even though there were other children around, the children were isolated. They did not play with each other. The attendants did not play with them or encourage play; they just sat against the wall talking to each other.

Depressed and anxious, I asked, "That child who is just lying on the floor, did he just lie on the floor when he came to Willowbrook?"

"No."

My perspective changed sharply. It does not take eighteen years of domination in Willowbrook to learn to be a catatonic. Even the youngest of children perceives and internalizes the lesson of enforced passivity and submission. From the very beginning, children learn that the most appropriate coerced action can be inaction.

What kind of thought can be modeled after inaction? How is a disabled child to grow up? The teacher I had spoken with earlier in the day told me that during their time out of class the kids just sat and did nothing. Now, like a shocking before and after picture, her words came true as the bell rang for class. Suddenly the same masters of nothingness I had seen just five minutes before now bounced, rolled, and ricocheted off the walls. With class about to start they were happy, zipping into classrooms. Now they looked like children. And they would be children, happy children, more or less happy anyway, for three or four hours. After that they would go back to the wards.

"How old are the children when they stop going to school?" I ask.

"About 13."

"What happens then?"

"Their whole lives become like what you saw in the wards."

I mentioned the building I now thought of as Maria's building. "Is that what becomes of them? Is that their future?"

"Yes."

I could have admired Willowbrook, a model "total institution" of humane domination and efficiency. But I was too horrified and afraid.

Willowbrook grafted itself to my life — not only what happened during those two days — but to me in my life as a person with a disability. I had witnessed how helpless, disabled subjects had been made into objects and I was angry. I headed back to New Haven to present my findings to the staff.

Ordinarily I have no trouble giving presentations. But preparing my staff presentation on Willowbrook and Washington gave me pause. Concerned that I might not be heard, I spoke with my friend Kitty MacKinnon, then studying for a Ph.D. in Political Science at Yale. Even then I sensed parallels between feminism and my experiences as a man with a disability. She immediately understood and agreed to witness the presentation.

The next morning, with Kitty observing, I gave my presentation. In the

same way the Yale faculty club had expressed disbelief at my father's experience of the camps after World War II, most of the staff denied the reality of
what I had to say. Impossibly, one staff member assured me that "Washington knows best." Another spoke clinically of the residents of Willowbrook as
if they were mere objects, asking, "How many of *them* per staff member?"

In those days, smoking was common. Feeling more and more nervous,
I took out a cigarette. Another staff member sharply reminded me that there
was no smoking at staff meetings. Suddenly, I realized that many regarded
me as one of *them*—a disabled person, an object. After the meeting, I asked
Kitty, "Did what I think happen really happen? I mean, did people not know
what to make of me? Did they treat me differently? Or was it my imagination?"

Kitty replied, "It happened. It wasn't your imagination."

A half hour later I was in Ken's office. "How," I asked, "am I going to
write a book for strangers if people I know refuse to acknowledge that there's
a problem here?"

In addition to being an excellent scholar, Ken was an excellent clinical
psychologist. I remembered his words to me when he had first brought me
on staff: *You have a way of making people comfortable with your disability.* Now
I understood that the weight of making people comfortable would rest almost
entirely on my shoulders. His words were exactly right. "What did you
expect?" he said. "The staff is young." We talked about youth and hang-up,
and then we cut a deal. I would work on this issue if I did not have to bury
my passion. Finally, I said, "I'll do the book, but I want a co-author."

"You find one that you're comfortable working with," Ken said, "and I'll
come up with the money."

In short order, I settled on John Gliedman, a pixie psychologist of enormous intellect who had written his Ph.D. dissertation on visual perception
only to see his topic put into practice in the bombing of North Vietnam. John
and I shared a sense of right and wrong and similar political views. Together
we produced a landmark book, *The Unexpected Minority: Handicapped Children in America.*

More than just about children, the book offered the first sustained soci-
ological view of disability, what the new field of Disability Studies now refers
to as the "new paradigm." Disability Studies considers its subject much as
African American Studies, Women's Studies, and Queer Studies do, as a potentially oppressed minority stigmatized by social power. The "cure" comes pre-
dominately through political action. *The Unexpected Minority* was an
ideological underpinning of the disability rights movement.

What had been an idiosyncratic view now became a common view. The

Americans with Disabilities Act overwhelmingly passed by Congress is explicitly predicated on the view of people with disabilities as an oppressed minority.

Much of my life before Willowbrook was concerned with the civil rights
movement, the anti-war movement, and the women's movement — and, from
time to time, with matters Jewish. As for disability as a social issue, it had
never seemed to me necessary or even interesting to identify with it. Psychologically emancipated, I was not politically emancipated. I found it hard to
identify myself as "disabled." Even harder was my new awareness of the filter
of loathing and shame through which I viewed my disability.

I still regarded my disability as a defect — not a social construct that I
might fight. The disability rights movement only makes sense if disability is
viewed as a social category. Without a social and political context, disability
cannot be understood as anything except a problem of medicine, bureaucracy, and charity. With a social and political reality, disability can be understood as part of the human condition much like membership in other groups
like blacks, women, Latinos, seniors, et cetera, that can be changed by political action.

The Unexpected Minority was the right book at the right time. I had
approached a non-existent children's movement and came out of it not only
with a children's movement but also a disability movement. I, who had never
had a connection to disability rights, now became part of this movement of
affirmation. And with that my own life and professional career changed.

With my attention consistently forced to disability studies, I had to make
a choice of the good over the beautiful. It was not simply a matter of coming out of the closet. It was a matter of mapping the space outside of the closet.
I contributed to and continue to contribute significantly to that mapping. This
is another satisfaction of my life; another thing I would do all over again.

Because New Haven was still an impossible place to meet women and
because of my love for the city, I moved to New York. I found a 2,000 sq. ft.
loft in Tribeca with a marvelous view of the Hudson. My roommate was an
art student named Valerie and my half of the rent was only $200. Three days
a week I commuted to New Haven on nearly empty trains running opposite
of the rush hour crowds. In New York I had many friends. My friend Gene
from Yale had moved there as had Margot Adler and Marjorie Katz from
Berkeley. Samia Halaby had left her job at Yale and lived a scant four blocks
away.

In 1975 I met Judith at a huge loft party in John Chamberlain's place
where we danced away the night. Judith was an artist who had a loft a few
blocks from mine and we spent much time together. By day I wrote and did

other work for Carnegie. Every Friday and Saturday evening we could be found at Fanelli's bar with friends and acquaintances, and usually afterwards we went to art openings and sometimes Soho artist loft parties. I came to make this life, Judith's life, my own.

This was in the days before Tribeca and Soho had been discovered by anyone save artists. From my apartment in Tribeca, I walked from neighborhood to neighborhood savoring the sense of freedom it gave me. To the south was Wall Street; to the southeast, Chinatown and then the Brooklyn Bridge. To the northeast was the East Village; to the north, Soho. In all that time and all that walking, I never encountered any problems that I didn't ask for. Thus, I was a fool when one day while walking next to the East River with Patricia Fink and her purse was snatched, I scampered after it and in two blocks I caught up to the kid who had snatched it along with a group of his buddies. An idiot out of breath, I panted, "May I have the purse back?" The surprised kids turned around with knives in their hands and handed me the purse. I said, "Thank you," and lurched back to Pat even more out of breath.

But that was the New York of thirty years ago. Today Soho is a chic area for shopping and Tribeca is the name of Robert DeNiro's film production company. My $400 loft is undoubtedly a co-op with a market value of over a million dollars. Some things, however, don't change. New Yorkers are still in too much of a hurry and too self-involved to stop and stare at me. Yet contrary to their press, whenever I have asked New Yorkers for directions or have otherwise arrested their movements, they have always been kind and generous.

When my job at Carnegie came to an end in 1976, I moved to the Institute for Research on Poverty at the University of Wisconsin at Madison and Judith moved with me. While I felt guilty for kidnapping Judith from her New York roots and transplanting her to Madison, her art thrived there. Although Madison, a third-rate Berkeley, left something to be desired, anything I wanted in my new job was generally provided. Here I produced another book, *The Handicapped Speak*, and several discussion papers with an approximate circulation of 2,000, several of which were republished in academic journals with smaller circulations.

In Wisconsin my mustache froze to my beard and the snow squeaked under my feet. But Madison, described as an all–American city by a glossy all–American magazine, was more than cold; it was so clean it made me feel like an uncomfortable dust bunny in comparison. Even the politics of Madison were squeaky clean. I yearned for a smudge of dirt. But then, I have always been anti-anal. Perhaps that is why I detest bureaucracies, pigeonholes, and other schemes of rigid classification that categorize me as "Disabled," "Jewish," "Radical," or "Other" bit of filth.

In 1978, my two-year fellowship in Madison over, I began another job search and went to Washington to see about a job recommendation from Patricia Wald who by then had become Deputy Attorney General in the Carter Administration. A month later, I told an FBI interviewer that I had been involved in the anti-war movement, which I suspect is why nothing materialized for me in Washington. Recalling my previous impressions of Washington, this was something of a relief.

I found myself with three job offers — one as assistant professor of political science at the University of Illinois at Chicago, one as assistant professor in the School of Social Work at UCLA, and one as associate professor of social welfare at the State University of New York at Albany.

Although the job at UCLA was the most interesting, the price of houses in Los Angeles would have greatly exceeded my salary and Los Angeles was far from the New York that I loved and to which Judith had ties. The Albany job paid double the Los Angeles job and housing was one-fifth the price. Judith would be only a short train ride from New York and we seriously discussed the possibility of living in New York once I got tenure.

The job interview at the University at Albany, State University of New York went well mainly because I was not attached to the outcome. That summer I plunked down $32,000 for an old Victorian row house in desperate need of renovation located right in the middle of downtown Albany and thus began a new era.

CHAPTER 25

A Pain in the Neck,
June 1989

I had fewer than three weeks until the radical dissection surgery: a little time, a little energy, so very little. But it was enough to attend my twenty-fifth reunion, enough to celebrate my forty-seventh birthday, and enough to make good on an outstanding promise to Daniel of a trip to Montreal. Because I was so weak, the trip was short. Judith came with us and the three of us had breakfast and dinner together. The days were Daniel's and mine. As weak as I was, I got to know him more closely and liked what I saw. Daniel fulfilled every expectation and dream that I dared have and many that I didn't dare have.

The third day we went to see the Montreal Expos play. In my youth, I had seen one major league baseball game. Daniel had seen none. On the way out to the stadium we both had intimations of this as a ritual between father and son. We got tickets. We walked a block to a small neighborhood restaurant where Daniel ordered a smoked meat sandwich, which he remembers as singularly delicious, and I remember as the sandwich that Daniel remembers as singularly delicious. We went back to the stadium.

Two-thirty approached and nothing happened. We had misread the time that the game started. I was too tired to make it to an evening game. The situation was ripe for disaster. Outside it began to rain. I found the nearest wall and sat on the floor, my back against it. I invited Daniel to sit down, and he slid down beside me.

"I'm really disappointed," I said. "I expect you are too."

"The schedule was wrong," said Daniel.

"No, we read it wrong," I said. "Let's just sit here and decide what we want to do." I was taking a gamble, a calculated risk. I wouldn't have expected most adults, including me, to entertain such a discussion in the face of such a disappointment.

Daniel said, "How about going to an amusement park?"

"It's raining. I don't think that would be a good idea," I said.

"What about a movie?"

"I don't think movies are shown in the afternoon," I replied.

"They have some pretty neat underground shopping malls here. We could try going to one of those until the rain clears up." This seemed agreeable, so we went off to the subway singing our walking music, the theme from *The Pink Panther*.

Back in downtown Montreal, we walked around the mall and shopped. By the time we found the perfect wallet for Daniel, it had stopped raining so we walked over to Chinatown. We bought a present for Judith and stopped in a Vietnamese restaurant for some soup. Then we walked back to the hotel. That night we went to a French restaurant. Daniel loved the food at the French restaurant as much as he had loved his meat sandwich at the little restaurant near the ball field and was convinced that Montreal had the best restaurants.

Daniel had carved a perfect day from a block of disaster. I admired his maturity, flexibility, and creativity. My son was wise. If he had to, he could live with me dead. Yet I knew that life would be much easier for him with me around. That was much of what had kept me going, and it would keep me going.

Back home in Albany, I finished preparing the ground. We informed the director of Daniel's summer camp and his counselor that I was being operated on for cancer, and I arranged for weekly phone calls with Daniel. I began work on a magazine article on computing and disability, which would occupy me for the next week. I said my goodbyes to people at the university. Daniel went to camp. Judith's mother came to Albany to be with her in case something went wrong during the surgery. My sister came from Washington to be with my mother and to run interference for me at the hospital. Against all my wishes, I had to change families to support myself during my struggle.

All systems were go. For the third time, I checked into Yale–New Haven Hospital. I had been an accomplice in the destruction of my body throughout the last two procedures. This was nothing compared to what was to come. By now I was a pro. Remembering my previous experience, I asked my mother to call a urologist to check if she could get the Coude catheter with its special soft tip. She could. I needed a 5cc balloon and we were finally able to locate three of them. As I checked into the hospital I told the resident who would be with Sasaki during the surgery about the catheter. So it was that I was wheeled into surgery with a balloon catheter with a flexible tip.

To my right was a small Italian girl who spoke no English. I squeezed her hand. Her tension dissolved into a smile. To my left was a patient receiving last minute words from the urologist who turned out to be the one my mother had consulted regarding my catheter. I said, "Thank you." The man turned around with a puzzled look on his face. When I explained what I was thanking him for, he said, "You're welcome."

When I was wheeled into the operating room, Sasaki asked, "Any questions?"

"No questions," I answered. "Good hunting."

While I was out, Sasaki sacrificed my internal jugular vein, the nerve to my trapezius, and a chunk out of the markedly developed mastoid muscle in my neck. Son sprinkled radioactive iodine seeds throughout my left neck and under my jawbone.

When I awoke some six hours later, my first words were, "What are my chances?"

The ugly mass had been about one inch in diameter. It had the nerve to adhere to my jawbone. Sasaki had cut off the sliver of mandible to which it had adhered. While most of the mass had gone to pathology, I had arranged for some of it to be mailed to a laboratory in California for in vitro tests on susceptibility to chemotherapy. I had discovered that if I had a tumor, in all likelihood it had developed immunity to the chemotherapy I had already undergone.

These in vitro tests were designed to find out what chemotherapeutic agents the tumor was most susceptible to. If the tumor was immune to one chemotherapeutic agent it had also developed immunity to a whole class of chemotherapeutic agents. I had become very good, even picking up points that had escaped my physicians and this testing was being done at my suggestion. There was much more than a psychological payoff in my regarding myself objectively as a case.

I was in the hospital for five days. The radioactive iodine implanted around the excision had a half-life of about eight days, which meant that every eight days it became half as potent. Unlike my last "seeding," these low intensity seeds did not require me to be isolated and friends and relatives flowed in and out of my room. Each morning Sasaki and the residents made rounds. One resident was assigned to ask me questions. As they left, Sasaki was always the last one out of the room. Each day I saved a single question for him. The first day's question was "Does involvement with the bone make things more serious?"

Sasaki answered, "Yes, it does."

On the second morning I asked Sasaki, "Would you recommend chemotherapy?" It was a loaded question. I knew that I wanted chemotherapy.

But Sasaki's answer would be an indication of how serious my case was. Sasaki answered, "We would certainly recommend chemotherapy."

Sasaki regarded my case as dire. The answer to each question showed that a serious procedure had been performed, and each day in embracing the most dramatic treatment, Sasaki was reaffirming the precariousness of my situation.

On the third day, quite unexpectedly, I took a trip to Son Valley, the radiation suite in the cellar. The trip had about it a quality rather like that of returning to a childhood time and place — perhaps Bantam Lake — where the odds for a happy ending had seemed excellent. I had been there for the first stage of my treatment when the odds were reasonable and when I would have been optimistic, if I had allowed myself. This time was joltingly different, a replay on an old, warped vinyl which threw off the needle. I was unprepared for this trip. The ride down was bumpy. I had not had a chance to drug my body so that it would be still for my CAT scan. On the way out I passed Son. The situation was painful to him too. His radiation that had achieved such elegant control of a local tumor had, in the end, failed. He said, "I told you that there was a forty percent chance of failure."

Back in bed in my room, I cried. I had gone back to a place of relative health, back to the beginnings. Everything had failed: first the radiation, then the chemotherapy, and then the functional neck dissection.

A social worker came into the room. Unlike Paulette, she did not have the instinct to simply hug me. She was hell-bent on quick psychotherapy to dry my tears. I did not need nor want psychotherapy now. I knew exactly why I was crying. I told her to leave me alone in an emphatic voice that she had to obey.

But the news was not all bad. Although I had brought with me an early portable computer in case I would not be able to talk after the surgery, luckily, especially given my abysmally awkward typing, this turned out to be unnecessary.

Warren Ilchman, then executive vice president for academic affairs at my university, came to visit bearing some lovely flowers cut from his own garden. Apparently he had talked with my mother or sister, or perhaps he knew that my situation was grave for other reasons. He said that the university was at my service and that I should attend to my own health with the assurance that my employment would be intact. I told him that I would like to teach as always.

Further, the surgery had not done as much damage as it might have done. My muscles were acting fine. Although Lew feared that the radical would negatively affect my dystonia, it turned out that it didn't. My head was not turned to the left. There was no uncontrollable tremor. Even the cosmetic effects of the radical neck were better than usual given the massive size of my neck. As far as the nerves to my trapezius, the effect was not really so debilitating. Had I been a bird, I would not have been able to fly. With the exception, as it would turn out, of putting on coats, my movement was not compromised. Lew was clearly pleased at this. I was too.

On the third day I took my first steps. Again, as with my previous surgeries, I had quite forgotten how to walk.

CHAPTER 26

Albany, 1978–1988

During those long sleepless thinking hours of cancer, I traced the crack in my office ceiling and organized and reorganized the strands of my life in various ways. Although some parts of my life remained confused, on the whole, it made sense. Further, I was pleased with it. I had done things that made a difference for me, my family, my friends, and for people whom I shall never know. As I traced my way back and forth between Vermont, Carnegie, Madison, and then, finally, to Albany, I was pleased to think that even had I known what would happen, I still would have done the same things. I still would have become involved in politics — still would have married Judith — still would have wanted Daniel as my son — still would have worked at a job that I loved.

Our house was located right in downtown Albany in the middle of a block governed by Mae Carlson, a Canadian who had moved to Albany during the Great Depression and had taken up prostitution as a profession. As she aged out, she became a madam and then a landlord. Now we moved onto a street inhabited by her former girls and their children. She delivered the votes on the block to the Democratic machine, which in turn delivered tenants on welfare to occupy the rest of Mae's buildings. Of course, the welfare checks went directly to Mae who provided the room and board.

Our block was something like a family, and, incredibly, it worked. When I visited her, Mae was in her eighties and living in a modest basement apartment with four refrigerators that were open to her tenants. She settled disputes as she chain-smoked Chesterfields without filters. When she died of lung cancer, three houses on our block caught fire. Having lost its mother, the family in our neighborhood on lower Lancaster Street disintegrated.

If Madison was too clean, Albany had more than its share of dirt as well as the oldest political machine in the country. Early on, I attended a taxation equity meeting with the assessor and Mayor Erastus Corning. The leaders argued with the assessor and won every argument. Mayor Corning rose from his seat in the back of the room. "I don't see what the problem is," he said. "Anyone who has problems with taxes can come and see me." The meeting dissolved and its participants went to talk to the mayor individually for personal favors. Corning was a master politician.

Our ornate Victorian townhouse was grand and beautiful and altogether in desperate need of renovation. My father expressed his misgivings about the house to my sister who tried to reassure him and herself as well by saying, "This house really has possibilities." And although it took me two long years to fully realize those possibilities, its rehabilitation was a clear source of pride to me, and I found myself an altogether capable general contractor.

In the midst of supervising the installation of new plumbing and wiring, new ornamental plasterwork, and the replacement of an ornate oak ceiling in the kitchen, I came up for tenure and we discovered Judith was pregnant. Amazingly, at the age of thirty-seven, I found myself facing fatherhood, a condition I had never even considered remotely possible. Under ceiling beams devoid of plaster, Judith and I were married in one corner of the living room — neither of us seeing any sense in marriage without children. Now tenure would not just affect my future, but the future of my son; I resolved to get it — and did. We rented a nearby apartment and Daniel crawled into the world on March 4, 1979.

Eight months later our beautiful new little family moved into our beautiful home and together we began writing a new chapter. We would have eight precious years before I was diagnosed with cancer. These would be eight years of rich family life and of demanding work and social life of the university community, the artistic community of Albany and our neighborhood community. There would be my father's death, and there would be the soulful satisfaction of being Daniel's father.

Although I had never been explicitly or implicitly trained for fatherhood, I was an excellent father and Daniel was an easy child. I knew enough about the subject of children to feel confident in throwing away the books, relying instead on instinct — mine and his. I took him on walks, with him in his backpack and me in my shoes. When it came time for him to walk in his own shoes, I made sure they had Velcro closures like mine because I found it impossible to tie shoelaces. Years later, my former colleague at Carnegie, Hillary Rodham Clinton, was to write of the importance of shoelaces and to come out against Velcro for her daughter.

Despite Daniel's physical strength and grace, as he grew, I was on a constant lookout for any turning of his foot. Although my parents were only too aware of dystonia, they did not discuss Daniel and dystonia with me, and Judith did not encourage discussion. For the most part, I kept my worries

Daniel as a baby in between me and my father, ca. 1982.

about this to myself and certainly never discussed them with Daniel until after he graduated college. Al Solnit approved of my painful deception. Dr. Flesh disapproved of my not telling Daniel that I had dystonia earlier. As far as I know, I was honest with Daniel about everything else including Santa Claus and the birds and the bees.

Not long after Daniel's birth, during my second year at Albany in 1979, luck struck. Warren Ilchman from my department of political science at Berkeley became director of the Rockefeller Institute and the first provost of Rockefeller College, of which the School of Social Welfare was part. We liked each other immensely, and he liked being a mentor. He recruited me to the newly formed department of public affairs and policy, and I served as its first chair from 1982 to 1984. Although it was his baby, I was there at its birth and even had pretensions at midwifery. I also had fun teaching in it.

I would be away from the School of Social Welfare for almost a decade. Looking back over those ten years, I can trace an arc that seems as dazzlingly sharp and pleasurably clear as a baseball heading over the fence towards a home run.

Of course, I maintained my ongoing devotion to the disability rights movement. In 1981 I attended a conference of national leaders in the disability rights movement and of members of the Washington civil rights community. The object of the Disability Rights Education Defense Fund was to establish a Washington office to press for voting accommodations for people with disabilities. It was the start of the Reagan Administration and there were rumblings about cutbacks in the civil rights legislation already on the books for people with disabilities. I did not think that we had any business turning our limited energy toward voting, a view shared by others who were in the Washington community. We persuaded the meeting to open a Washington office of DREDF dedicated to preserving and enhancing existing legislation instead of directing efforts towards voting. This strategy proved necessary and correct. Patrisha Wright, who later would become known as the mother of the Americans with Disabilities Act, was the director of the Washington office.

In 1982, I attended another meeting of national leaders in disability and of the then nonexistent field of Disability Studies. The meeting took place at Wingspread, a mansion turned conference center designed by Frank Lloyd Wright. I am not aware that Wright ever designed a comfortable chair and this was true of Wingspread. With the exceptions of Harlan Hahn and Paul Longmore who had the prescience to bring along their own wheelchairs, everyone was uncomfortable. At the end of the meeting, we were all called upon to make a commitment. I committed to make computing technology accessible for people with disabilities.

In the same year, I set about writing a book about public policy toward the arts that was an expansion of a previously published article, "Art and the Market." As I started my research, hypotheses emerged rapidly, and I was on to an exciting and promising piece of research, analysis, and prescription. As I started writing, however, the manifestations of my dystonia created a familiar frustrating filter to my research efforts. First, I could not write on the research cards because I cannot write with my hands and the writing that I could do with a ballpoint pen between my teeth was too slow and too messy. Then, because of the ways that my fingers and hands moved and sometimes jerked, handling the hundreds and sometimes thousands of cards was cumbersome and they usually ended up on the floor.

There had to be an easier way. I soon found there was.

Even in 1983 the technology existed to let me search for articles electronically, and to write and re-write using word processing, et cetera. I reasoned that if parts of writing were difficult for me, there must be parts of writing difficult for other people with disabilities. Working on the assumption that someone must have already solved this problem, I made some calls to people with disabilities and organizations of them throughout the country. To my surprise, with a few exceptions like the TRACE lab at the University of Wisconsin, I could not find any organizations that knew about the use of such technology by people with disabilities.

In 1983 I applied for and received a small grant from my university to follow through on my commitment to investigate the application of computing technology to people with disabilities. I was also given access to resources at the Institute for Governmental Studies at the University at Albany. My research project coincided with the mission of the Rockefeller College for Public Affairs and Policy, a sub-unit of SUNY Albany, where I teach. I began to envision a Center for Computing and Disability that would serve not only college students at SUNY Albany, but also people with disabilities, industry, and the public sector within and outside of New York. By now the disability rights movement had appropriated the word "disability" and the word "handicap" was as inappropriate as "Negro" or "girl."

After six months of research I became convinced that substantial technology already existed. What did not exist was the social mechanism to make the technology available to people with disabilities. The problem was more the political and organizational one of creating arrangements so that people with disabilities might be matched to appropriate computing technologies. Traditional keyboards could be replaced with head paddles, tightly grouped keypads, light responsive sensors and devices that allowed control with a blink or a puff of breath. In a few decades, the very concept of disability could be radically changed and all persons with disabilities would be able to work.

Changing course, I now set aside art and public policy and took up the organization of matching technology and disability. In 1984 I established the non-profit Center for Computing and Disability at SUNY Albany and began looking about for funds. During the first year, I was unsuccessful. I knocked on many doors, wrote many letters, and generally drove myself crazy. By the end of the second year, as a result of changes in technology, personnel and private and public interests, the nation had changed. People were ready to hear what I had to say. All the groundwork I had previously done to develop the Center now began to pay off. Around this time, Warren introduced me to Hank Dullea, Governor Mario Cuomo's Director of State Operations, and we wrote the Center for Computing and Disability, perhaps my most significant organizational contribution, into the state budget as a continuing item.

In 1986 Governor Cuomo and his excellent staff had inserted a paragraph into his State of the State message:

> One way to alter attitudes about disabilities and simultaneously to help people with disabilities realize their full potential is to see that they have access to the complete array of society's technological advances. For many persons with physical

and developmental disabilities, the Year 2000 has already arrived. The computer, for example, has a special service to perform for persons with disabilities, and its applications are beginning to become known to people who are blind, visually impaired, deaf and hearing impaired. But the pace of technological change in this field outstrips the organizational, social and entrepreneurial modifications required to bring these powerful tools to people with disabilities.

Prior to the Center being written into the State of the State message, I had submitted a proposal to the Federal Office of Education. Although they had declined our first grant application, the second almost identical application in 1985 was approved.

Now we received funding of over $300,000 in 1980s money.

I wrote a letter to John Akers, then CEO of IBM, requesting an executive loan that would extend into August of 1988, and Governor Cuomo signed it. Suddenly, the Center for Computing and Disability was a going enterprise and was instrumental in Governor Cuomo's Task Force on Technology and Disability in 1987. I remain grateful to the Cuomo administration for believing in me. I trust that by now their belief has been repaid in service to New Yorkers and other people with disabilities.

In 1987 the Center for Computing and Disability was well underway and soon had a national, state, local, and university presence, and I achieved national recognition in the field. Now well beyond the stage of entrepreneurship in 1988, the Center for Computing and Disability was on its feet and toddling and I was a proud father. At peril to my university career, I had thrown myself into the Center because it was worthwhile and good.

Then one evening Daniel said, "Hey Dad, your breath stinks!" and everything changed.

CHAPTER 27

Dancing in the Street, June 1989

During my time in the hospital for the radical dissection, I had developed a reputation as a fighter. But once home, it was clear to me I had been in the ring much too long. I couldn't do much more than hold on to the ropes and breathe. Three days after I returned to Albany I was still holding the rope but starting to breathe with my diaphragm when the phone rang shortly after five in the afternoon. I answered on my speakerphone.

"This is Dr. Sasaki. I have good news for you. I called in for the pathology report. There is no cancer."

I did a bona fide doubletake and fell to the floor. I had always thought before that doubletakes were only creations from the movies. I got back on my chair. "Could you say that again?" I asked. My voice was weak from the radiation and the surgery.

Sasaki said, "There is no cancer."

"What was that mass you took out?" I asked.

"Not sure. But it was not cancer."

"Thank you. That's wonderful. I'm thrilled!" I exclaimed.

I ran downstairs and out to the stoop of my downtown row house where I persisted in sitting long after the days when it had been fashionable. Now I sat down and pronounced, "I beat it!" My exclamation turned into a chant, each word receiving its own emphasis. "*I* beat it. I *beat* it. I beat *it*. *I beat it.*"

I was ecstatic.

I ran upstairs and telephoned my mother. "Hello?" she answered. I knew her voice well enough to know that she was trying to keep up her spirits.

"There was no cancer," I said.

She must have done her own Viennese doubletake. "What did you say?" she asked. She did not trust her hearing. I placed my mouth closer to the

157

speakerphone and spoke slowly and deliberately. "Sasaki called. He got the pathology report. There is no cancer."

"My God!" she said.

I called Lew and told him. He said, "If they did thorough biopsies of so much tissue it seems to me that you're in the clear now."

I agreed. I had been over-diagnosed and over-treated and the radioactive seeds gave me an insurance policy. Ordinarily I might have felt resentful about this. I did not. I was ecstatic.

I called Rick who had asked a venerated orthodox rabbi, the Lubovicher Rebbe, to pray for me. Rick's explanation was simple: it was a miracle.

I called Gary. He was overjoyed. His explanation was that the biopsy had been a false positive.

When Judith came home, she found a maniac on the front steps chanting, "I beat it. I beat it. I beat it." She would have been perfectly justified in thinking that I had lost my mind. She said, "Beat what?"

I answered, "Beat the cancer. Sasaki called. The pathology was negative. I am free and clear." Judith was speechless.

Family and friends reacted in one of two ways. One was to be overjoyed, as I was. The other was to regard the radical dissection surgery as unnecessary. Indeed, there are two logical explanations. One, the needle biopsy I had just before the Yale reunion was a false positive. Two, the needle biopsy had been a true positive and in the time between the biopsy and the surgery a miracle had occurred. I entertain the miracle explanation because I am a sucker for bribes. I will not believe in a God because I am told that I need him, but if he does me a favor ... well, maybe.

The members of my team subsequently delved hard into this matter and came to the conclusion that given a positive needle biopsy, it would have been irresponsible not to throw everything at the cancer. And although I would lie if I did not express my displeasure with a radical, risky and unnecessary surgery, there simply was no way that any of us could have known that it was unnecessary.

A week later Fisher got a call from the laboratory in California. The lab had been unable to culture cancer cells, another confirmation of there being no cancer.

CHAPTER 28

After the War, 1989–1990

After the war, I needed time to absorb the shock of living again.

The surgical procedures, the radiation, the chemotherapy, the constant alertness, the roller coaster life for somebody who loves walking, all had worn me thin. I lost eighteen pounds, largely muscle. My stamina was low and I was taking an unconscionably long time to recuperate.

In June after Daniel was promoted from the fifth grade, the two of us undertook to complete our earlier abbreviated trip to Montreal. Although I was still weak and wobbly, we had a magnificent and memorable time and, among other things, got to see the Montreal Expos play and, just for us, win. In the middle of the seventh inning, as is tradition, Daniel and I stood up, looked at each other, and stretched.

Either Daniel had changed or I had gained a new appreciation for what it means to be at the beginning of life. But whatever it was, inexplicably and naturally, I found myself regarding Daniel as another adult. Not that he lost his innocence and childhood; he still possessed both. And he still liked child-like things. Yet with the exception of twenty minutes over a table in China-town where he persisted in flicking a Chinese yo-yo at me, he acted like a proud adult.

The Center for Computing and Disability was in its third year of growth and influence when my cancer was diagnosed. Exhaustion made my customary seventy-hour weeks at the Center impossible. Fighting for my life, tired or depressed or both, unable to eat, and unable to sleep, I had no energy left.

One day as I was getting ready to leave for New Haven for a biopsy, I was saying good-bye in the secretary's office when a colleague said in a friendly Freudian slip, "Good luck on your autopsy." I hesitated only a moment before assuring him, "I have no intention of having an autopsy."

Although the Center was anything but a one-man show, without me it stopped growing. As I watched the Center abort, shrink and wither, I decided to choose my fight. It would be with the cancer.

The year proceeded.

Some three months into autumn, a curious thing happened: that heightened alertness left me. I no longer woke up in the middle of the night afraid of my cancer, thinking of what to do next, reflecting on what I had done. Although rational in its time, my hyper-alertness was now irrational, and I had to turn it off. I did. I stopped dreaming of cancer. Indeed my dreams became pleasurable; and a good thing, too, because now I slept ten and eleven hours a day.

Although I bore disabilities from my cancer treatments — chewing hurt; my dry mouth hurt; I could only speak softly, et cetera, et cetera — it was damned good to be alive. I had changed. I understood myself and other people as never before. Not only were my perceptions agonizingly clear, my understanding was as well. I shed the chaff and held the wheat ever closer to my heart. My insight was dazzling.

In December, my Aunt Hertha, who had been relatively healthy six months before at my forty-seventh birthday, now rapidly grew desperately ill. As the cancer metastasized to her bones, I went to New Haven for a checkup and while there arranged with a doctor friend of my father's, for her to receive more intensive medical supervision. The odds for her being present at my funeral had been in her favor. Now, in a twist of irony, I witnessed her death.

Still tired and weak, I celebrated New Year's Eve of 1989 by writing letters. One letter was to my mother and one was to Daniel whose copy I asked Judith to keep with the other letters and the videotape I had made earlier for him in case of my death. The last was a letter of thanks and appreciation to the members of my team and to other people: Ronald DeConti, David Fisher, Evelyn Fogarasi, Lewis Levy, Steven Parnes, Daniel Roth, Judith Roth, Stefanie Roth, Clarence Sasaki, Gary Saxonhouse, Albert Solnit, Yung Son, and Richard Sugarman. The letters were written partially in fear that I might die before I had the chance to express the contents. For the rest, it was a straightforward proclamation of joy and thanks.

In my letter, I wrote:

> Each of you was necessary for me to live into 1990. For that privilege I owe you each a profound debt, my life itself. Each of you has contributed differently and knows the nature of your contribution. This list should no doubt be longer. The day when Richard Ruiz came to my room and stopped the bleeding will always be a reminder to me of the thinness of the line that separates life from death. I ask Doctor Sasaki to share this memorandum with the rest of his skillful and caring staff. I will not forget the wisdom, intelligence, skill, judgment, and kindness you displayed. Indeed, I have learned something of these qualities from you. You were not only necessary to my life but inspired and inspiring teachers.

Cancer has made me blunt and direct. I can do no otherwise than express my gratitude.

Spring of 1990 was a joyful time of new life. I was still weak, but getting stronger and able to get out more. Every corner of the universe awoke and burst into bud. Albany blossomed with tulips and spring flowers. On June 1st came another birthday — my forty-eighth. My mother came up from New Haven, and we had a party at my cousin Diane's who had just moved to Albany with her husband, Robert. I had a cake full of candles to blow out and lots of help to do it. The comparison between this birthday and the previous funereal ones was obvious. One thing was the same, however. I cried, as did others. Only this time we cried with the possibility of my life on the horizon.

CHAPTER 29

Press Pause, 1990–2000

Press pause. Breathe for two years.

During these two years, Daniel moved from fifth grade to seventh; Judith and I divorced; I watched the Center go down; and I moved out of my beloved home to an apartment down the street. I deliberately chose the apartment for its proximity to the house, which meant that Daniel never had to leave the neighborhood of his friends and made it easy for him to walk back and forth. My sister Evy came up from Washington, and within days she set up my apartment with a talent I did not know she possessed. I came to love the apartment, which had a huge living area and two bedrooms, one for me, the other for Daniel.

After the divorce and during my long recovery from cancer, Daniel and I lived together in our apartment during the week. We were the oddest of odd couples. I looked to Daniel to do things for me that I could not do for myself. As I lacked the fine motor control required to handle sharp knives and hot pots, Daniel rapidly became an accomplished cook of a limited repertoire. We shared glorious meals of perfectly broiled chicken breasts, pasta al dente with olive oil and spices, and huge Tupperware buckets full of our version of Kim Chee, which we made by slicing Chinese cabbage and punching it with our fists in the tub. Then we added olive oil, vinegar, cayenne pepper, Tabasco sauce, and whatever else we could find. On the first day it was good, by the fifth day it was marvelous.

In many ways Daniel took care of me and felt responsible for me. Although I wish it had not been that way, the fact of his care was substantially true and his amazing grace with that responsibility was a tribute to him. When we played chess he would move my figures. At times I could have imagined that he read my mind by observing my body. Further, he trusted me sufficiently to know that I would not ask for his help unless I needed it. I never used the word "dystonia" with him, referring rather to "my disability." I am sure that he noticed the stares of others and discussed my disability with some of his friends, but he never told me of that. Nor did he ask me why I was different from other fathers. After all, I was the only father he ever knew.

The years we spent in our apartment were a difficult time because of the cancer and the divorce. Still weak, I was nonetheless able to get myself to classes at the university where I taught classes on computers and disability. Because many disabled people took the course, I was able to teach the course from the social and political minority group perspective, the creation of which was partially my doing. Out of class, I sat in the sunshine, watched my son play baseball, breathed, and savored episodes of grateful tears. I made some friend-

Daniel the chef, 1990.

ships in my apartment building and much enjoyed leaving repairs to the landlord. Then one evening at a party I met Carol whose radiant warmth immediately attracted me. Press play.

Almost two years after the radical dissection and radiation, I was diagnosed with a soft tissue necrosis or gangrene in the neck. My ENT man in Albany removed it under the lightest of anesthesia, but the necrotic soft tissue he removed left me with a hole in my neck the size of a tennis ball. A couple of hours after surgery I was as high as a kite on opiates and bandaged like a bunny. My new love, Carol, Daniel, and Rick came to visit, and we had a raucous time. I bounced up and down on the bed in high spirits.

Several days later I returned to my apartment with a wound that would not heal. The more it hurt, the more opiates I downed. I hit the big leagues when I graduated to an extra strong Fentonyl patch. Not only did the opiates take care of the pain, they took care of any concern I might have had about my life. I was a junkie floating in paradise as the wound did not heal but grew. When my mother came from New Haven to visit me, she took one alarmed look at my blissful face and said, "Billy, you are dying!" I did not feel like I was dying; I was far too high. But my mother knew a misbehaving wound when she saw one.

I called Lew who made an appointment for me with Yale's former chief of plastic surgery, Stephen Aryan. Carol drove me down to New Haven and Lew drove us to Aryan's office. Had I not been so high I would have questioned what I was doing there; I had always associated plastic surgeons with nose jobs, facelifts, and tummy tucks. But now, however, I was so high I would have agreed to a boob job.

Carol, 1990.

Aryan took one look through the opening in my neck and said, "Your carotid artery is about to blow. I give it about two weeks. I can try bringing up a flap from your chest. I will have to bring up an artery because in radiated fields like your neck there is insufficient oxygen. I'd say the procedure has a fifty percent chance of working."

Fifty percent beat certain death. With a new appreciation for plastic surgeons, I took the gamble and went into the hospital. On reflection, I had nothing to lose so it was certainly not a gamble. During the nine-hour procedure, Sasaki patiently debrided the carotid artery that fed the left side of my brain and removed the necrotic part of my mandible. An oral surgeon gave me four root canals from the inside. Finally, Aryan brought up a myocutaneous vascularized flap from my chest and under my clavicle to fill in the hole in my neck, which resulted in my having to shave the chest hair on my neck. As usual I had a copy of the operative reports mailed to me. These were especially horrifying. I later learned that Aryan had developed this procedure and was among the most successful with it.

All of that long day and evening, Carol, Daniel, my sister Evy and her husband Andre kept vigil in the waiting room. The surgery had been long and the anesthesia heavy. My mother used her old faculty ID from the Yale Medical School to get into the recovery room. When I would not wake up she must have thought I was going up to heaven. In my hospital room, one of my nurses who had trained with my father not only took good care of me but also instructed the other nurses to treat me especially well. Long after his death, my father was still taking care of me.

Three days after the operation, with Daniel holding me up by the hand, I took tentative tottering walks down the hall. After each stay in a hospital bed it was as if I had to relearn walking. I basked in Daniel's love and Carol's love and the love of my family who had seen me through my cancer treatments.

Now my post-cancer-war life moved into a period of relative calm. To an outside observer, these years would appear less eventful than my pre-cancer life. This is partly due to my lack of energy, which is a result of the cancer therapy. For the rest, it is the result of my increased age, my change of vocation in which I focused more on teaching, reading, and writing, and my attention to parenting Daniel into adulthood.

Daniel's childhood was a combination of urban urchin mouse and country mouse thanks to his attendance at the remarkable Farm and Wilderness Camp in Vermont where he subsequently returned as an adolescent counselor and teacher. Daniel was a precocious athlete. He swam, danced, skated, and flipped balls with the greatest of ease and grace. I loved to watch him play pick up football and baseball in the field between Jay Street and Hudson Street. Perhaps my attending to his lessons like an apprentice scientist had something to do with teaching Daniel that he had worthwhile things to impart to other people. I sat at a deliberate distance on a Jay Street stoop across the street and watched his grace, his smarts, the marvelous ability he had, and still has, to get kids to work and play together. I watched to admire him, and I watched to enjoy him. Finally, I watched to protect him and to be there in case something happened, which sometimes it did.

As Daniel entered adolescence, my parenting entered a new phase. Carol and I moved into a large apartment together with Daniel who spent weekdays with us. After I moved out, Daniel and his gang threw a party in the empty apartment. Daniel's friend Leon advertised the event on the Albany High School bulletin board. The party turned into a raucous rumpus, and a girl put her foot through the living room wall, which resulted in the confiscation of my security deposit and my recognition that big kids could get into big trouble. Throughout his teenage years, Daniel stayed out later and later. He broke curfew after curfew. Finally I was reduced to one curfew he could not break, "I insist that you be asleep before you wake up!"

Since Daniel was now of driving age and because our new apartment was a mile from his old neighborhood, this gave him a transportation problem and me feelings of guilt. In order to assuage this guilt, I bought him his first car, a used Honda. Carol, with her purist's predilection for stick shifts, taught him how to drive on her stick shift.

I naively thought cars were used for transportation and that Daniel would use the Honda to get to and from school and to and from his old neighborhood. But I discovered that the main use of the car by adolescents is to socialize. Daniel routinely packed six of his friends into the car, turned up the stereo, and went for rides that brought up the odometer on the Honda sometimes a thousand miles each week. Had I but known, I would have got him a moped, maybe even a sports car with two bucket seats. As things were, I now not only had a son to parent but a car.

Daniel and his car had a parting of the ways. The car was packed and the stereo was on full blast. Some of the occupants were smoking marijuana, and the rest got contact highs. Everybody was bopping, and a police car spotted them, pulled them over, and took them to the police station. They all went to court, and our lawyer copped a plea. At court, I discovered that a third misdemeanor is a felony under New York state law, and I saw poor people charged with felonies. Daniel had the luck not to be poor, but his insurance was revoked and, at that, I sold his car and he went without one until he was twenty-two.

As painful as these instances were, they were isolated experiences in a wonderful coming of age. In the fall of 1996 Daniel entered Gallatin College, a small liberal arts college, which is part of NYU. There, Daniel's natural leadership and passion for the environment soon led him to a self-designed major in community organization and environmental issues.

A few months after Daniel entered college, when the December cold and snow plastered Albany and I was on my winter break, Carol and I eloped to Puerto Rico. We made no advance plans, but we knew we would return married. Long experience has taught me that many wonderful things happen if one does not make specific plans. I have been through more than enough planning in my life to love the magic of spontaneity.

You have only to set the stage for magic, not write the script. Carol was in the mood for enchantment. We spent our first week exploring Puerto Rico, cutting across the island past the impressive radio telescope that listens for extra-terrestrial intelligence and winding up on the south side of the island. Here there was an island of terrestrial lizards and a bay that glowed at night. On our way back to San Juan we traversed the magnificent mountain spine of the island. Soon we became lost on roads that became ever narrower, and endangered by the small trucks laden with coffee beans that sped down them.

Carol and me around 1994.

In San Juan I telephoned Carmen, a one-time neighbor from Albany, who had introduced me to the *curandaro* who had chanted over me when my cancer was at its most outrageous.

"Hello, Carmen," I announced. "I would like to get married."

"No problem," replied Carmen. "I know a judge."

"I knew you would know what to do," I said.

Carmen took the next day off from work and guided us to the place of marriage licenses. Following Carmen's counsel, I tipped the man. Driver's licenses were available at the next window, but I declined the opportunity to get my first. A half hour later at the judge's office we were married. Carmen treated us to an extra special, super delicious lunch and our "lucky" lizards joined us in our hotel room for the honeymoon.

While schnarfing around San Juan, we noticed a small sign off to one side that said in Spanish "Wholesale chocolates." I do not speak Spanish, but I am fluent in the French version of Spanglish. "Let's go inside," I said to Carol. Inside was stuffed with expensive chocolates at wholesale prices. Carol spotted a bouquet of chocolate roses, and I bought a dozen to give to Carmen.

In 1997 Carol and I bought our house in Albany from whose second floor office I dictated this book. Close to the university and medical centers, the house is a smaller version of the New Haven house in which I grew up — and in a similar neighborhood.

After the Center on Computing and Disability crashed, I went back to teaching at the School of Social Welfare from which I had been absent for more than a decade and found myself with a new taste for writing. In addition to the usual academic articles, I completed many of the draft notes for this book as well as an unpublished dystopian novel that incorporated my experience and that of Daniel and his gang. I also wrote *Personal Computers for Persons with Disabilities* (McFarland, 1992), *Letters to Daniel* (Creative Arts Books, 2002), *The Assault on Social Policy* (Columbia University Press, 2002), and was a contributing editor to *Globalization, Social Justice, and the Human Services* (State University of New York Press, 2007).

After Carol and I were married, I made Daniel a standing offer of an annual two-week vacation with us. During these vacations and in the times between, Carol, Daniel and I made up a new family, which Daniel handled superbly. He did not speak about Judith to us or about us to Judith. Of course, Judith and I spoke with each other, particularly about Daniel, and we both had the sense not to let the causes of the divorce into our current life. Although I am under few illusions that the divorce was not painful for Daniel, much less than that it was better for him, still, we all made the best of it.

Our first vacation together we went out West. In Las Vegas we rented a car and drug dealers offered to sell Daniel weed and cocaine. We made a large circle including Hoover Dam, Lake Mead, Bryce, Zion, and the Grand Canyon. Dazzled by the beauty of Bryce and Zion, our eyes were fully opened by the time we hit the Grand Canyon, which surpasses its name. Although it was in the middle of tourist season and we had not made any reservations, a room became available right in the middle of Grand Canyon Village. The next day the car was covered with snow. A couple of days later, the three of us were schnarfing away down the legendary Route 66.

Long ago I put aside the tourist delusion of the grand tour. I design vacations with a general route and a maximum of "schnarfing" time. Although you will not find the word in your dictionary, schnarfing is the art of singling out the remarkable in the mundane, the unusual in the ordinary, the hidden in the cave of the hider. In short, to schnarf is to live. For example, when Daniel and I went to London, I had a few destinations in mind: the Elgin Marbles ripped off the Greek Parthenon, the British War Museum that was the bunker from which Churchill and his staff directed operations during World War II. For Daniel there was the changing of the guard, the wax museum and of course 221B Baker Street. Aside from these planned sites, we had only to schnarf to find bliss. The first magnificent result of schnarfing was the duck pond in the park adjacent to Buckingham Palace. We found a bench and sat ourselves down for what proved to be the whole afternoon. There were ducks of all sorts, some swans and even some loons; an uncommonly long neck here and fake large eyes there. Bipedal, many walked in even more inventive ways than I.

When I showed Daniel and Carol my Paris some years later, we schnarfed the men in green who cleaned the streets, the way the buildings glowed in the jet-lagged dawn, the existence of French windows instead of the rather stupid double hung windows. On a later vacation to the northwest, we schnarfed a gorgeous sunset and witnessed the rare and instantaneous green flash on the Oregon coast.

When Daniel was twenty-one and spending his last semester of college in Spain in the spring of 2000, our roles were reversed and it was he who guided Carol and me around Spain. He would be our guide, our porter, our interpreter, our selector of sights, in short, our host. He met us at the airport in Madrid and when we arrived at our destination, Carol asked him how much of a tip to give the taxi driver. Daniel said with surprising authority, "No tip. He overcharged us."

Daniel's apartment in Madrid was in a commercial neighborhood reminiscent of New York's east village during the time I lived there in the late '60s and early '70s. There were posters on some exterior walls, elaborate graffiti on others. At night the prostitutes and pleasure seeking young people took over the streets and Daniel noted that the police actively protected the prostitutes.

Daniel was a particularly generous host, and he swept out the apartment and did the wash. There is a certain thrill to watching one's son clean out his apartment for your benefit. As I had shown him France, Daniel now showed me Spain. It is a tribute to both of us that we can play it both ways. How Carol adds herself to the mix is a tribute to her. We all agreed we wanted plenty of time for schnarfing. Beyond that, I wanted Daniel to see Picasso's masterpiece, *Guernica*, and a bullfight and Carol wanted to see some flamenco. Daniel purchased tickets for a performance and then left us to sleep while he went out to enjoy the nightlife that often runs to seven in the morning.

In Spain, the main meal is at mid-day. Dinner is usually around ten o'clock, and impossible before eight-thirty. Daniel introduced us to the *menu del dia*, an appetizer, an entree, a dessert, wine.

At ten o'clock, we went to the flamenco of Juan Cortes, dancer, organizer, and choreographer of a performance called "Soul." Cortes would turn out to be a celebrated exponent of a modern flamenco influenced by modern dance, Broadway, and, in a certain sense, jazz. Cortes is certainly conscious of the meaning of "soul" in jazz and in calling his performance that claimed the same for flamenco, even in his modern version, the music of the Gypsy. Cortes' subtext had some certain similarity between the Roma or Gypsy and the African American, a display of the importance of the Gypsy to the Spanish version of machismo, sexuality and death. We all found the machismo irritating, particularly Carol who called it unforgivable narcissism.

The next morning the three of us paid homage to *Guernica*, Picasso's stunning rendering of the Basque city bombed by the fascist Franco in 1937 during the Spanish Civil War. Guernica was the first aerial bombardment in history whose target was a civilian population and whose apparent intent was total destruction. For the German Luftwaffe, it was an experiment and trial run for the coming tactic of blitzkreig.

The Franco years are a large void in the consciousness of contemporary Spain. Daniel pointed out that young people his age had little continuity with their parents who had grown up and lived under Franco. There were some generational differences in our family as evidenced in Daniel's surprise at my interpretation of *Guernica* as commentary on total 20th century war.

Madrid was in the middle of one of the country's countless festivals. Daniel bargained with a scalper for tickets to a sold-out bullfight. We entered a circular stadium and sat on hard stone ledges. The bulls did not naturally want to fight, and required substantial torture to make them do so. Everything—even the cruelty—had an order to it, an order that Daniel noted is characteristic of much Spanish culture.

Even outsiders like us could appreciate at least some of the skill of the matador. The crowd waved fans. The interaction between the crowd and the matador was as structured as that occurring within the ring. We the audience were part of the spectacle. Then I realized that what we were watching derived from the Roman gladiators. We all noticed similarities between Cortes and the matadors, the dance and bull fight, including some Spanish interpretation of death. We left the bullfight after three bulls, disgusted, as we suspected we would be, but glad we had come.

Spain is less one country than, say, England or France. We drove from Castillian Madrid up to the industrious Basque country and down to the Mediterranean Catalonia. Even the countryside had Roman, Moorish and Catholic ruins. Spain is not only spatially diverse; its complex history is visible in its architecture.

After three days I gave up trying to understand Spain.

Barcelona, in Catalonia, was in the middle of a festival, and the cultural center had a flamenco concert that night. We learned something about flamenco as we witnessed it in its purest form with two people sitting down, one with guitar, one chanting. The music was and was not tonal. Flamenco was not Spanish but Gypsy. The concert was in the courtyard of the cultural center, open to the sky where a high wind pushed the clouds. The music of the *Cante Jondo* moved us profoundly, particularly Carol, who was converted from a flamenco fan into a flamenco purist.

During this marvelous trip, I distinctly noticed that my walking felt different. Some strangers seemed to notice as well and they gave me an unusual amount of space. I began to take cabs for even short distances and found myself stumbling on the cobblestones in Barcelona. While exploring one of the ancient caves with superb paintings near Altamira, I could not walk on parts of the slippery jagged floor and Daniel carried me.

CHAPTER 30

Return to Dystonia,
2003–2007

Like an imperial lord who reappears at the gates of the kingdom many generations later, dystonia now crossed the border and again began to annex territory. The small stumbles and staggers I'd noticed during our summer excursion in Paris, and later more acutely in Barcelona, now became more spectacular. At school I found myself slamming into walls and stumbling and falling. My colleagues and students either did not notice or pretended not to notice except when I fell, when I became the center of attention. But I had been friendly with the ground ever since high school when I had lived so close to it. I still knew how to fall without getting hurt, and my standing up was part of the same motion as my falling. By the time someone said, "Are you all right?" I was upright and on my way. Since going up and down the stairs of concrete and steel with clever ledges well designed to snag my feet made falling more frequent and potentially dangerous, I grabbed the handrails tightly. Further, my balance seemed off. True to myself until the end, I managed to pretty well ignore all this. I did, however, go to Albany's movement disorder clinic and requested injections of Botox to the nerves that caused my left foot to curl under. The botulinum toxin had no noticeable effect.

Later that autumn in 2002, when Carol and I went to my family's Thanksgiving Day dinner at my cousin Ernie's house in New Haven, I called Lew Levy and asked if he could see me. "Sure," said Lew, and gave us directions to his new office in the suburbs.

I was silent at the family Thanksgiving Day dinner because ever since my cancer I cannot talk while eating. A new generation of Roths sat around the family table replacing the Roths who had died. My cousin Ernie was the only European-born Roth left, and it was at his house that the family gathered after my mother aged. I did miss Daniel and my niece Simone who, as children, had become like brother and sister but without the baggage. Daniel was on his island off the coast of the state of Washington as the Lopez Island Community Coordinator, and Simone was now an overworked resident in pediatrics. Present at the table too were my deceased ancestors, particularly those who had been around my mother's table for earlier Thanksgivings: my father, Oscar, Uncle Walter, Aunt Hertha, Uncle Rudi, and my grandfather, Arthur, not to mention my many ancestors who never made it to the Thanksgiving table. Also present was my mother who had died six months before at the age of ninety-one.

Over the last three years of her life as my mother became frail, I saw her often. Whenever I asked, Carol drove me from Albany to New Haven and, when I didn't ask, she urged me. My family referred to Carol variously as angel and saint, and my love for her, if possible, became deeper.

Intent on spending the end of her life in her own home, my mother resisted my sister's urgings to enter an assisted living residence near my sister's home. As my mother became weaker, she developed an increasing dementia, most probably due to a series of small strokes. My niece, Simone, naturally evolved an effective way of communicating with her; she simply lay down in bed with her and hugged her. I learned the lesson and did the same.

Daniel and Simone, 2004.

On heavy doses of opiates for the excruciating pain in her back, my mother often complained at waking up from a recurring dream where she was with her mother and my father in the heaven she much preferred to the painful reality. In the spring of 2002 she had a massive stroke and died in a coma at the same hospital where my father had worked and died, and where, in the hallway just around the corner from her room, hung an oil portrait of my father. I was shocked when fewer than fifty people appeared for her memorial service until I understood she had outlived most of the people in her generation. In the years before her death, we exchanged many letters in which I expressed not only my love for her, but also my admiration. As a European Jew she had escaped from hell while half her family and six million Jews did not. She was the last living family link to a magnificent generation and an amazing people.

Partly because of my mother, I am aware of my debt to women. As Goethe said in *Faust*, "The eternal feminine draws us onward." Accordingly, I dedicated *The Assault on Social Policy* to three women: my wife, Carol Chisholm Roth; my sister, Evelyn Roth Fogarasi; and my mother, Stefanie Zeimer Roth.

With my mother and Evy, 1987.

Towards the end of her life with her death in mind my mother sent me a letter in which she wrote:

> I know that you all will be sad. But I want you to think about my very long and very wonderful life. I've had everything a person can ask for: good health, good looks, a good mind, a wonderful husband, wonderful children and grand-children, great parents especially a most wonderful mother who unfortunately died too young. I was always surrounded by good friends, and had a profession I liked and many enjoyable interests. It was a hectic time in the world, but we were very lucky overcoming it all.
>
> I never had that destructive love of money — so when I did not have any money, it did not destroy me, and when I had it I was not unhappy to share it. How much more can you ask for!
>
> One of my greatest treasures in my life was a son that was able to become a wonderful man despite unbelievable obstacles. I love you, I love your Daniel and your Carol and I admire what you achieved in life. Stay well darling and stay the way you are, although you could be a little less of a dictator.

With the death of my mother, my sister and I no longer felt a filial obligation to live for her sake. From now on, I would live my life for its own sake.

The morning after Thanksgiving was cold and clear, and it was with some trouble that Carol and I found Lew's new office. Now seventy-five, Lew was still as sharp a neurologist as he had been the first time I saw him during my senior year in college. When I asked if he wanted to know what the neurologist in Albany thought, he snorted and said, "No. I want to examine you myself."

Lew dismissed my Botox treatments and, concerned by my stumbling gait, twisting neck, and other dramatic changes in my dystonia, gave me a particularly thorough neurological examination. When he was done he strongly recommended that I consider a form of brain surgery called deep brain stimulation (DBS). The surgery was serious, strenuous, and experimental; serious because all brain surgery is serious; strenuous because it would take some fourteen hours during ten of which I would be awake; and experimental because there were few people with dystonia on whom it had then been used, and many fewer with prior lesions such as mine. This proposal struck me as reasonable. After all, less dramatic interventions were doing nothing to halt the progress of my movement disorder.

My future life demanded that the surgical team be as experienced, skillful and brilliant as possible. And although Lew did not feel comfortable recommending surgeons, he was more than willing to "make himself smart" one more time. And so was I.

Back home in Albany, I started snooping the internet. I discovered that

the DBS operation was a sophisticated form of the surgery that I had undergone some forty years before with Cooper. In that time, Cooper's reputation
had risen from that of "near quack" to that of "pioneering genius." New ways
of imaging the brain had evolved — particularly the MRI, which assists in
visualizing the brain — and microelectrodes make it possible to listen to individual cells. They had also discovered that a high frequency voltage was as
effective as creating a lesion thus making the surgery safer and reversible. Of
course, computers were involved in all of this, which made deep brain stimulation more of a science and less of an art. And the target for dystonia had
changed. Cooper's target had been the thalamus, now the target was the globus
pallidus.

Over the next year, as my dystonia steadily became more severe, I continued with the Botox injections. But in a matter of months it became clear
that the injections were not working. I also continued to explore the internet and my research and Lew's friend netted us the same name: Andres
Lozano, the first-rate neurosurgeon who headed an impressive surgical team
at Toronto Western Hospital. I wrote for an appointment and they scheduled
me for an evaluation on June 10, 2004. Although I hate being judged, I hated
waiting five months for judgment even more.

They declared me a fit candidate and scheduled the surgery on November 14, 2004. The five-month wait was an agony made all the more difficult
by the continued progression of my dystonia. In August I had a root canal
that didn't work. My jaw became infected, a clear contraindication for surgery. Once again I split in two. I asked my dentist to take an X-ray, which
revealed a dime-sized lesion in my jawbone where the root canal had failed.
She called her favorite oral surgeon who squeezed me in. Ever since the cancer radiation my jaw is liable to disintegration, so I called Dr. Son, the radiation therapist. "It's over ten years, you should be in the clear," he said. The
oral surgery removed the infection, but then the stitches broke. Had I not
internalized my father, I should simply have become a nervous wreck. As it
was, I was dead calm, but calm waters hide turbulence. The wound did not
heal, and I faxed a letter to Lozano explaining my situation, sure that I would
be rescheduled and deferred while my dystonia galloped. But to my astonishment, Lozano replied, "We can go ahead as scheduled." And so it was that
I appeared in Toronto on antibiotics with an open healing wound. The roller
coaster was back in business.

I am a keen judge of doctors, and Andres Lozano struck me as one of the
best. An attractive young man in his forties with straight black hair, Lozano
is simply one of the best functional neurosurgeons of his generation and has,
in fact, trained many of the functional neurosurgeons in North America.

Unlike most academic physicians, Lozano was surrounded not by a roost of residents but rather by a flock of fellows who had already done their residencies in neurosurgery and were now training in this super duper specialty of functional neurosurgery under the tutelage of the master.

Lozano is a brilliant surgeon with a genuine humility whose conversations with me have been uniformly informative and warm. Lozano knew his medicine, and he also knew as much as anybody about dystonia. "You are unique in several ways," he said. "Fewer than a hundred people with dystonia have had DBS. You are the oldest person with dystonia on whom we will operate. We have only operated on one other person who had prior lesions. And it is unusual that dystonia does not plateau at some point. Yours is getting worse." I was so unique, in fact, that a fellow on the team wrote a paper about my surgery, which was presented at a poster session during the next movement disorders conference in Rome. As with Cooper's surgeries, most of the team's procedures were performed on Parkinson's patients. And as with Cooper, no one knew for sure how and why the procedures worked when they did work. "Make a plan of what you'll do if your dystonia does not progress as well as a plan for your life if you become bedridden," Lozano added.

Other members of the Toronto team included Elena Moro, the movement disorder neurologist specializing in deep brain stimulation who would program my DBS device. At the time, she was the only neurologist in North America formally trained in deep brain stimulation as well as in programming the computerized gizmo that would be implanted into the new bionic me as I became a cyborg. The neurophysiologist who would advance the probe and listen to the cells was also top flight. These three doctors and more than ten other people would be required to work together in the operating room as a team. I found all of them immensely likeable. I dwell on this because all a patient can do is choose physicians who are up to doing the job and I had to be certain that I had settled on the best. That the team in Toronto was also loving and compassionate was an extra bonus.

For the necessary five-week stay after the surgery, Carol and I rented a two-bedroom condominium in Toronto. The five weeks were so that Elena Moro, M.D., Ph.D., the Italian *maestro*, could make countless adjustments to my bionic implant from a range of even less countable possible combinations. The second bedroom in the condo was for the family members who stayed close by all during those weeks: Daniel, Evy, Andre, and Simone from my side and Carol's sister, Patti, her niece, Renee, and her brother, John. The surgery was a family affair and Carol and I were never alone. Aside from having each other, at least one member of our family was always with us.

To prepare for my ten hours of waking surgery, I had taken classes in meditation. As Daniel is something of a master at this, the night before the surgery, Daniel and I meditated together and I felt myself absorbing his youthful strength. Although I could feel guilty about being such a vampire, I knew he didn't mind. By this time my dystonia had progressed so that I could no longer walk nor eat by myself. Carol fed me and pushed me about in a wheelchair.

The next morning before dawn, I checked into Toronto Western Hospital flanked by Carol, Daniel, Simone, Evy and Andre. They stayed close by me as my head swelled with massive amounts of a local anesthetic. As the team screwed the stereotaxic frame firmly into my head to establish a coordinate system, despite the anesthesia, I could feel the pressure of the screws as they invaded my skull. Whatever their feelings, my family kept their emotions inside them and did not add to my burdens by sharing them.

Then my surgical team took over. There were some ten people in the operating room. Each knew the particulars of their specific jobs and each of them knew how to work together as a team. I actually saw only four of them. The others were behind the drape that had been put over my head to provide a sterile field. I heard the drill as they made two holes in my head. Although I was an old hand in stereotaxic surgery, this did not make it any more agreeable. And although I tried to meditate, I was too uncomfortable to achieve any consistent success.

Then Dr. Lozano set the trajectories to a precise part of my globus pallidus, which is located deep inside my brain right next to the optic nerve. I heard talking from behind the drape but could barely decipher it. In front of the drape were Dr. Moro, super surgical nurse Yu Yen Poon whose assignment it was to take care of my every need, an off and on anesthesiologist, and a mysterious figure in the distance who seemed to be taking notes of what happened throughout the procedure. It was Yu Yen who did most of the talking and also took care of moistening my mouth, which had been dry since the cancer radiation.

As the electrode approached my globus pallidus, everyone including me listened to the amplified sounds of each cell in my brain. The sound was like radio static, which changed according to which cell the electrode was in. When Lozano and the others did not hear the sound they wanted, they repeated the process twice. While lying there, I idly wondered what the surgical team did about eating and urinating during such lengthy procedures. This second time they heard the sound of a globus pallidus in distress. Bingo!

"Close your eyes and tell me when you see flashes of light," Dr. Moro instructed. As she stimulated my brain with small escalating surges of electricity, it was as if I were looking at beautiful purple fireworks exploding in silence. Finally I saw nothing except at very high voltages. The team then repeated the same exacting procedure on the other side of my brain. When everyone was satisfied, they filled the holes in my head and stapled my incisions. Then with uncharacteristic formality, Lozano introduced me to the electrophysiologist who had advanced the electrodes who had the improbable name of Dostoevsky. For the next two hours I was asleep as the team threaded wires from my skull through my neck and down into my chest where a small computer and battery was implanted that could deliver rhythmic electrical pulses. At about the sixth hour, a neuro-physiological team took forty-five minutes to perform the research to which I had previously agreed.

When I woke up in my room in the neurosurgical ward, the first thing I saw were three commandments neatly written by Daniel on the large whiteboard that faced my bed.

1. Beware of wolves.
2. Never laugh at a giraffe.
3. Don't sneeze at bees.

I made up these commandments when Daniel was a child and insisted that he follow them growing up. In part, I suppose that this showed my contempt for easy rules. Yet they transcended themselves. I understood these three commandments as temporary role reversals and simultaneous affirmations of our father-son relationship. Curiously, each nurse who read them had distinctly different reactions. One shouted as if these were the words of the devil. Another giggled. Dr. Moro said, "It's probably a family thing."

After three days in the hospital in the continuing rotating company of Carol, Daniel, Simone, Andre, and Evy, who was as watchful as she had been earlier during my cancer hospitalization, finally I was sprung. For the first week, I slept twenty hours a day. I was not sick or tired; I was exhausted. Carol was angelic. I knew she was worried and even scared, but with me she was strong, loving, and competent. In fact my whole family operated together as a team. Even now, remembering Simone's presence during my surgery prompts me to tears because, I am ashamed to say, I did not expect it, and because her presence reminded me of my mother in whose steps she followed as a woman physician and with whom she had been so close. Daniel's presence was a given, so much so that I never had to thank him for it. Of course I was — and am — completely grateful, but such gratitude is not expressible in words, rather in actions.

Over the next five weeks after the surgery, I saw Dr. Moro three times a week. Simultaneously warm and businesslike, Dr. Moro is a quick-moving physician with shoulder-length black hair who knows her stuff backwards and forwards. A superb clinician and up-and-coming researcher, she is also a compassionate as well as passionate physician. When I posed the possibility of my dystonia progressing, she exclaimed, "Then we will fight it!" Each time I saw her, I appreciated her abilities more. Each time she increased the amplitude of the gizmo in my chest, we watched and waited with curiosity and excitement to see what the results would be. It was odd and a bit disconcerting to feel my body change with each tweak and adjustment.

Our condominium was in the middle of downtown Toronto. Once a stuffy English city full of tasteful if boring architecture, Toronto is now a thoroughly international city whose contemporary citizens give it not only tone but vibrato. Were it not for the miserably long and fearfully frozen winter, it would be a first-rate place to live.

A week after my surgery, Gary and his wife, Arlene, who are blessed with the most nearly perfect marriage of anyone I know, came up from the University of Michigan for a visit. We shared an appreciation for art and visited the Toronto Museum to view an exhibition of art deco. I have always had a particular fondness for this period of decorative art when so much seemed possible. Gary pushed my wheelchair and we stopped before each piece for a long while. I marveled at the clean beauty of a piece of furniture here, a tea set there, a beautiful set of tiles. Although I was enjoying the exhibit, my head ached from the air that had penetrated my skull during the surgery. Gary's face had filled out, and his frequent smiles twinkled. I knew that his life would be much longer than mine. But in the fall of 2006, he would die with intelligence and courage of a fatal cancer, even with the best of care. I can only imagine Arlene's loss. As for me, a rock in my world crumbled. We went back to the condominium and exhausted, I went to bed.

Gradually my exhaustion gave way to mere weakness, and I consistently used the wheelchair I inherited from my mother. Since I slept so much, the days passed quickly for me. Doubtless, time crept at a more deliberate pace for Carol and whoever else happened to occupy the second bedroom. Every Monday, Wednesday and Friday, the occupants of the condominium all went with me on visits to watch Dr. Moro as she increased the voltage in the bionic addition to my body.

November 2004. Thanksgiving again, but it was not a Canadian holiday. When Carol, Daniel and I discovered that none of us particularly liked turkey, we took ourselves to Toronto's Chinatown and gave ourselves over to a glorious Thanksgiving feast of Peking duck.

Only a year before my surgery, Columbia University Press had published my book, *The Assault on Social Policy*. In it I had written a chapter on health, which advocated a Canadian style single payer health system. Now I had a chance to experience this system, and found that substantially it works. I never experienced any bureaucratic problems with the Canadian healthcare system, and certainly all the physicians I met were more concerned with medicine than with money.

In a predictable but exasperating twist, in the long months of recovery from the DBS surgery, my health insurance company refused to reimburse me for the expense. My secretary, Ellen Burke, a high-caliber professional of the sort who holds large organizations together, got fighting mad. As I was often too tired to fight, I now took my turn working for Ellen as she kept track of countless rejections and wrote innumerable responses. Each rejection seemed to renew Ellen's energy. In the end, of course, we won our claim for close to $60,000. Ironically, this was about half of what the cost for the same surgery in the states would have been. Now whenever anyone asks me the name of my lawyer, I always reply, "Ellen Burke."

In the spring of 2005, in the midst of the bureaucratic insurance war, my painfully slow recovery, and the continual recalibration of the computer settings attempting to stabilize my body movements, my cousin Ernie died of lung cancer. Ernie kept his cancer a secret until he became dramatically symptomatic and then treatment was gruesome and relatively short. Ernie had been like a brother to me and to my sister, Evy, as well as to his own sister, Diane. Husband to Helene, and father to Eric, Mark and Glenn, he was also a familiar figure in New Haven where he had been vice principal of Hillhouse High School. As my mother was the last of her generation of Roths to die, Ernie was the first of his generation, my generation, to die. Because of my new speech problems resulting from the neurosurgery, I asked Daniel to deliver the eulogy I had written with the thought it would prepare him to give the eulogy at my funeral.

Earlier in that year I had attended the service for my colleague, Janet Perloff, who had a particularly nasty form of breast cancer. Throughout the years of her cancer, I never saw Janet cry with the exception of one visit to me during which she talked about her death, her son without her, and what her future might hold. Having both experienced cancer, we found it easy to talk about these difficult subjects. She handled her cancer with heroic intelligence and worked at her job with brio and gusto. Although I was an inspiration to her, she surely inspired me. Another colleague, beautifully named Dawn, became deathly ill. Perhaps she had given up, but she had not consulted anyone outside of Albany. I exhorted her to get a second opinion in New York. She did and today is very much alive.

Carol's father had a cancer of the prostate sufficiently advanced so that his urologist was urging invasive experimental treatment. I advised him to get a second opinion at Johns Hopkins, which has the best urology department in the country. He did and was told that the proposed treatment was insane. As events developed, he did not undergo the agonies of aggressive treatment. At the age of seventy, Joe died peacefully in his sleep from the consequences of a heart attack.

No matter what the situation, during these and many other conversations, I have uniformly urged others to take an active part in their illness. Now with Google, ignorance is a dangerous luxury.

Indeed, the World Wide Web and modern search engines are changing the doctor-patient relationship. For example, choose a drug and look it up on the net. All drugs have side effects. It is not that a relatively safe drug doesn't have side effects; it is that the probability of side effects is small. Learning how to judge and spot quack websites and sift through paragraphs and sometimes pages of possible frightening side effects to sort out useful probabilities requires some detachment and effort. But if you're sensible, taking an active and positive role in your own treatment has now become vastly easier.

Today I am cured of cancer. It is not in remission; it is vanquished. The absence of having experienced cancer in my life is as inconceivable to me now as the absence of my birth, my disability, my heritage, as the absence of Yale or Berkeley, or the absence of Daniel or Carol. My cancer cure has not been without consequences for the rest of my body. I once weighed twenty pounds more than I do now, all of it muscle. I once was physically strong, and when necessary, I was nimble beyond my dystonia. In short, I was a crippled hulk with a certain physical beauty.

The treatment necessary to save my life was enervating. I tire easily and sleep much. My neck is scarred and my voice is weak and distorted. Making myself understood is difficult. My DBS surgery had the rare side effect of considerably worsening my speech to the point where I often need Carol as an interpreter even though I make a point of placing myself as close to my listener's ear as possible. As a consequence of the radiation for my cancer, I always have water nearby to keep my dry mouth going in conversation, and Carol leaves a bowl of opened chewing gum on the kitchen counter so that I can get gum myself whenever I need it.

I am much more dependent on others, but this is far less upsetting to me than it would have been without my history of disability. Often I ride in a wheelchair. I miss walking and talking freely, indeed not being able to do so is a painful loss since both are important in an active social and political life. People are newly solicitous of me, and although I can't say I'm grateful for it, I have become tolerant.

For many years, my job at the Center for Computing and Disability was to come up with solutions to problems of disability for others. Now, as then, I make accommodations that ease the relationship of my disability to my environment. As I get older, this becomes more difficult. It came as something of a shock to me when a student recently referred to my gray hair. The last time I looked, it was brown with a few white flecks. The social consequences of old age are often even more profound than those of disability, and rare is the person who does not become disabled in late life. Aging and disability share biological and social similarities. Biologically, both make functioning in an able-bodied world more difficult and both require modifications to that world. Velcro closures are a perfect example. As a child, my son had the same Velcro closures on his shoes that I used on mine — as do many old people, who may also use canes, walkers or wheelchairs for mobility.

Over the last several years as my dystonia has progressed, I am no longer able to fasten and unfasten even Velcro closures. When I am at home, I am always barefoot because I am frequently in front of my computer, and use my toes to operate a large track ball placed on the floor under my desk, which provides endless entertainment for our cat who apparently regards the track ball and my toes as a real mouse.

My changing body has also caused me to make other adaptations in my clothing. Recently on the internet I tracked down cotton pants with elastic waistbands. I retired my suits and neckties to the back of the closet, never to be worn again. I am grateful for this, as my opinion of suits and ties has not changed since college.

Because I love my work and have no intention of retiring, I will be buried with my boots on and have requested that Daniel buy me a really fancy pair of Western boots for the occasion. Hopefully he will be able to find a pair with Velcro closures. My funeral attire, in Jewish custom, will also include a burial shawl. The prospect of this ensemble pleases me.

The changes and adaptations go on and on.

My mind is still sharp; perhaps it has even been sharpened. The internet has vastly expanded my world. I wake up each morning around five o'clock and spend a couple of hours online. I trade URLs with friends, particularly so with John Gliedman whose interests and politics remain as close to mine as they were when we met in New Haven during the Carnegie years.

My work environment has improved immensely due to the inspired leadership of a new dean. I see students at my home, which is also where my secretaries come. Our house, though hardly as grand as my one-time Victorian mansion on Lancaster Street, is quite likable and I recently had handrails installed to make it easier and safer for me to navigate the house.

My ability to speak was substantially impaired by an unanticipated

John Gliedman, 2007.

problem during the DBS surgery. Before this, I lectured freely. Now when I do lecture, Carol interprets and I insist on class discussion. Further, I use books that I have written to convey what I want to say. Strangely, student evaluations of my courses have improved. Perhaps this is because my students like teaching themselves. Or perhaps they like my teaching. Or perhaps it is because they like Carol so much. Or perhaps it is out of pity and admiration. *I will never know.* But in truth, I am long past caring.

The accessibility requirements for my life have also changed. During the summer of 2005, Carol, Daniel, and I set out for our first vacation since my DBS surgery. For the first time, global warming was real and the weather we left behind was beastly hot and rainforest humid. After driving around Yellowstone for two days, Daniel commented, "I understand why we're driving, but I can't understand why almost everyone else is. This park is for hiking." Of course he was right, and the only time I got out of the car was at the established sites that had paths that were accessible to the wheelchair that I now often use. I got around mainly by driving, but also by hobbling short distances, often leaning on Daniel and sometimes being carried by him, or in my wheel chair. As exciting and dramatic as our vacation was, Daniel said, "This is the last time you can take this kind of vacation. It's just too strenuous." He was right.

All these changes in my body and my environment require adjustment but as my sister said with an admiration reminiscent of my mother, "If anyone can do it, you can."

And I can.

Some eight months after my DBS surgery and just a few days after my sixty-third birthday, Carol, Daniel, and I returned to Toronto to see Dr. Moro to adjust the settings for the computer implanted in my chest. There are thousands of ways to adjust the programming and Dr. Moro is an experienced genius at this. Carol and Daniel were with me in the room as she cogitated and then changed the settings. Because each change takes a day for the effects to become noticeable, we spent that afternoon at the art museum inspecting a show of New York color field painting, old friends from my youth. The next morning and the next we were back with Dr. Moro for an hour while she recalibrated the settings. By the end of the third day she had made what seemed to my uneducated mind some radical changes, and my dystonia was less severe, my movements a bit more precise. Because a DBS system has thousands upon thousands of settings, and because it's a long drive to Toronto, I arranged with Dr. Moro to keep her informed of my responses to her new settings by e-mail. She then e-mails me prescriptions for new settings, which my Albany neurologist, Donald Higgins, is kind enough to follow using Albany Medical Center's DBS equipment.

For most patients with my brand of dystonia, DBS works dramatically. But ever the singular exception, my own results have been somewhere between modest and negligible. This may be due to my age at the time of surgery. Lozano guessed that the prior lesions placed by Cooper some forty years earlier disrupted the circuits around which DBS romps. One of Lozano's fellows suspects my dystonia started to progress again because of my cancer surgeries. Or it might have been from a long fever that I endured after radiation. Or perhaps it was the

Daniel, 2007.

chemotherapy. Or maybe it was just plain bad luck. As Dr. Moro informed me some two years after the surgery, it was even possible that the procedure had made my dystonia more severe in some respects. And of course, it is entirely possible that my long hours on the operating table did, in fact, work to arrest the rapid progression of my dystonia. Whatever the reason, what I do know for sure is that my life has been saved over and over again, and I enjoy living it.

For many years, the possibility of Daniel developing

dystonia was an agonizing secret and an abiding dread to me. My particular kind of dystonia runs in families and was once thought to be the product of a recessive gene. But when Daniel was five, a paper was published that said the gene was dominant which meant that Daniel had a fifty percent chance of inheriting it from me. I kept this information from Daniel until he was twenty-two and was almost certainly too old to manifest dystonia. In May of 2006, in his twenty-seventh year, my fears evaporated when a newly developed test proved Daniel did not carry the gene. There was absolutely no chance of his passing it on to his possible future children. It will end with me.

My weakness increased. It should not have. This was not dystonia. But my dystonia had caused my neck to twist and turn ever since I was a child. Throughout the next years, it began to appear that something was amiss with the part of my spine that runs through my neck. My spine was pressing against my spinal cord, a compression myelopathy. Many people over 50 have some problem with that part of their spine. I do not know what my future holds, but this is true of many other people who are 65 years old.

Another rock in my world trembled when, just before my birthday in June of 2007, my sister Evy telephoned, and announced that she had breast cancer. She caught it early, and it was treated with a lumpectomy, radiation, and hormone therapy. Of course, like any sane person with cancer, she has times of fear. Like Gary and me, she has the sense to act in their presence,

Daniel and me, 2003.

and she does her research. Her odds of remission are excellent. Unlike me, she had the decency to wait until after our mother's death.

Being certain that I have done my best is a source of profound satisfaction. I am certain I did all I could to save my life from cancer. I am certain I am doing everything I can to further my life with dystonia. I've done everything possible to play the odds towards life and against death. I have given myself every chance and edge for a good life. I am further more than content with my life, which is a gift conceived in love, built on a foundation of luck, will, and intelligence, and grown into a life of love and some small consequence.

How I love life and the people in it.

I am not afraid of death.

More importantly, I am not afraid of life.

Index